BROTHER TO ALL

The Life and Witness of St. Charles de Foucauld

Edited by

JOSEPH VICTOR EDWIN, SJ

ORBIS BOOKS
Maryknoll, New York 10545

ORBIS BOOKS
Maryknoll, New York 10545

Fathers and Brothers
MARYKNOLL™

Founded in 1970, Orbis Books endeavors to publish works that enlighten the mind, nourish the spirit, and challenge the conscience. The publishing arm of the Maryknoll Fathers and Brothers, Orbis seeks to explore the global dimensions of the Christian faith and mission, to invite dialogue with diverse cultures and religious traditions, and to serve the cause of reconciliation and peace. The books published reflect the views of their authors and do not represent the official position of the Maryknoll Society. To learn more about Maryknoll and Orbis Books, please visit our website at www.orbisbooks.com

Library of Congress Cataloging-in-Publication Data

Names: Edwin, Joseph Victor, editor.
Title: Brother to all : the life and witness of Saint Charles de Foucauld / edited by Joseph Victor Edwin, SJ.
Description: Maryknoll, NY : Orbis Books, [2022] | Includes bibliographical references. | Summary: "Essays reflecting on the life and witness of Charles de Foucauld (1858-1916) who has recently been declared a Catholic Saint"—Provided by publisher.
Identifiers: LCCN 2022003122 (print) | LCCN 2022003123 (ebook) | ISBN 9781626984844 (print) | ISBN 9781608339464 (ebook)
Subjects: LCSH: Foucauld, Charles de, 1858-1916.
Classification: LCC BX4705.F65 B76 2022 (print) | LCC BX4705.F65 (ebook) | DDC 282.092 [B]—dc23/eng/20220404
LC record available at https://lccn.loc.gov/2022003122
LC ebook record available at https://lccn.loc.gov/2022003123

BROTHER TO ALL

Contents

Introduction

Dear Brothers and Sisters:

This volume is dedicated to the life and legacy of Charles de Foucauld (1858–1916), a hermit and contemplative who died in a remote village in Algeria. At the time of his death, he was quite obscure. His dream of attracting followers was unfulfilled. And yet in time his story and his model of spirituality attracted interest and followers around the world. Many believe his model of contemplative life and "presence" among people of other faiths makes him one of the great spiritual teachers of our time. Beatified in 2005, he was canonized as a saint in 2022. Even before this event, Pope Francis singled him out in 2020 in his encyclical *Fratelli tutti* as a model of "fraternity and social friendship."

The contributors to this volume include contemporary students and followers of Charles de Foucauld, both scholars, missionaries, religious, and lay people, all exploring aspects of his life and message, and attempting to assess his inspiration and meaning for our times. At the outset, I invite you to listen to the words of Cardinal Walter Kasper, as he emphasizes the exemplary relevance of Charles de Foucauld for Christians and Christianity in the world of today. He said: "Charles de Foucauld seemed interesting to me as a model for achieving the mission of Christians and of the Church not just in the desert of Tamanrasset but also in the desert of the modern world: the mission through simple Christian presence, in prayer with God and in friendship with men [and women]."

Charles lived in a small hermitage in a remote village in the desert of North Africa, attempting to emulate the "hidden life" of Jesus in his years as a carpenter in Nazareth. The vast expanses of the desert can both amaze and frighten us. Both the silence and the whistling winds can inspire us and raise our hearts and minds toward our creator. The oases one may find among the shifting sand dunes may fill us with hope. Yet the words of Cardinal Kasper remind us there are other deserts in our contemporary world. They may not involve literal sand dunes, but in other ways men and women today live disconnected from one another. While we are created to care for one another, we fail to nourish the "culture of care." Foucauld, in contrast, lived that "culture of care" as a universal brother by living as a brother to men and women in the desert. He himself became a human oasis by his presence and friendship among his neighbors. We too are called to do the same in whatever deserts we inhabit.

Foucauld's life ended in the desert in a painful way. It might appear to readers that his life ended in failure. He neither "converted" anyone nor "attracted" followers. His story was not a story of success in terms of the "missionary mindset" of his times, or even of our own day. Reflecting on the apparent failure of Foucauld, Cardinal Kasper says: "The Jewish philosopher and theologian Martin Buber has said that success is not one of the names of God. Jesus Christ also in his earthly life did not have success; at the end he died on the cross and his disciples, except John and his mother, Mary, distanced themselves and abandoned him. Humanly speaking, Good Friday was a failure. The experience of Good Friday is a part of the life of every saint and every Christian."

Foucauld remained a hidden treasure for many years after his death, until a few men and women began to learn about his spirituality and drew inspiration from his witness. Today several religious communities of men and women as well as lay associations follow his spirituality. These men and women bring to the world a new dimension of service with their presence, love, and care. Elsewhere what Pope Francis said in a conversation with Austen Ivereigh is applicable to the mission of the spiritual sons and daughters of Foucauld: "The Church's role is played out in the service of the Lord and the peoples of the earth where she is sent, not by imposing or dominating but as Christ does, in the washing of feet." This is a message that applies to all Christians, whatever their setting or condition.

There is another aspect of Foucauld's example that bears special relevance today: specifically, his invitation to live among Muslims in friendship and solidarity, as brothers and sisters. Foucauld's own religious conversion was deeply inspired by the example of Muslim piety, and his life calls us to appreciate how many of our Muslim brothers and sisters "continuously live in the presence of God," our Creator and Master. For those who have come to know and appreciate our Muslim brothers and sisters it is very painful to see how the richness and immense resources of the Islamic tradition are ignored, distorted, and disdained by so many Christians today. This is another way in which Foucauld's message challenges us today, and his example is of great help to many Christians who engage with Muslims.

This is a particularly urgent challenge where I live, in India, which is passing through critical times: politically, socially, and religiously. The politico-religious narratives marked by exclusion, hatred, and discrimination continue to push India into a quicksand of communal disharmony. More than ever we need the example of men and women like Mahatma Gandhi and Mother Teresa, whose narratives of nonviolence and compassion are real antidotes to violence and hatred.

Pope Francis, in his encyclical *Fratelli tutti*, On Fraternity and Social Friendship, described Charles de Foucauld as one such person whose deep faith, drawing from his intense experience of God, "made a journey of transformation toward feeling a brother to all." Pope Francis reminds us that Blessed [now Saint] Charles prayed for the grace that he be a brother to every human being and asked a friend to 'pray to God that I truly be the brother of all.'" The pope writes: "He wanted to be, in the end, 'the universal brother.' Yet only by identifying with the least did he come at last to be the brother of all. May God inspire that dream in each one of us."

In their various ways, the contributors to this volume have been inspired by that dream. May their reflections help to inspire others to learn more about this great saint of our time, and so to pursue their own dreams.

Joseph Victor Edwin, SJ
Feast of Saint Ignatius of Loyola (July 31, 2022)
Vidyajyoti College of Theology, Delhi, India

1

Charles de Foucauld: Acrobat of God without a Net

Leo D. Lefebure

Charles de Foucauld presented multiple, shifting personae to the world, ranging from a spoiled, overweight, agnostic aristocrat nicknamed "Piggy," to a mysterious wandering Jew, to a gaunt, underfed Catholic ascetic with a penetrating gaze. Again and again his decisions placed his life in danger; but, as his biographer Jean-Jacques Antier commented, "'Security': that was the least of Charles's concerns! Acrobat of God, he chose to work without a net."[1] His path was unconventional and often problematic, and he worried at times that he was not accomplishing anything of value. A restless heart kept driving him until he found a place in the desert where he could rest in the heart of Jesus.

YOUTH

Charles-Eugène de Foucauld was born into a wealthy, aristocratic family in Strasbourg on September 15, 1858. Among his earlier family were legendary figures like Bertrand de Foucauld, who died fighting under King St. Louis of France in the battle of Al-Mansurah in the Seventh Crusade in 1250, and Armand de

---

1. Jean-Jacques Antier, *Charles de Foucauld* (trans. Julia Shirek Smith; San Francisco: Ignatius Press, 1999), 147.

Foucauld, the vicar general of the Archdiocese of Arles who died as a martyr of the French Revolution in the September Massacres of 1792. Charles's father, the Viscount Edouard de Foucauld, held a position inspecting forestry in Strasbourg. Both of Charles's parents had died by the time he was but six years old, and he was raised by his maternal grandparents, Colonel Beaudet de Morlet and his wife. When war between France and Prussia began in 1870, the colonel realized that Strasbourg was endangered; and he moved the family first to Brittany and then to refuge in Berne, Switzerland, before finally settling after the war in Nancy.

Charles's mother and then his grandparents gave him a very pious upbringing. Nonetheless, as an adolescent Charles questioned whether we could know anything of the reality of God, and by the end of 1874 he had lost his faith. He later described this period of his life in a letter to his cousin Marie de Bondy, "At seventeen, I was all egotism, all impiety, all desire for evil; it was as if I had gone a little mad."[2]

Studying with the Jesuits at the Sainte-Geneviève School in Paris from 1874 to 1876 did not restore his faith. Intending to continue the military heritage of his family, in 1876 he entered the military academy Saint-Cyr, where he came to know many students who would become leaders of the French Army in Algeria and World War I, including Philippe Pétain. These contacts would be important during his later time in North Africa. When Charles reached his twentieth birthday in 1878, he inherited a considerable fortune both from his parents and his grandfather, and he proceeded to spend it in pursuit of pleasure. As a young man in the army, he was a wealthy, overweight viscount in love with wine, good food, women, and the luxuries of this world; his lavish lifestyle earned him the nickname *Le Porc* ("the pig" or "Piggy").[3] He was graduated from Saint Cyr next to last

---

2. Charles de Foucauld, Letter to Marie de Bondy, April 17, 1892; cited by Antier, *Charles de Foucauld,* 31.

3. Antier, *Charles de Foucauld,* 50.

in his class, but he went on for further military studies at the Cavalry School in Saumur. Both as a student and as a junior officer, he was repeatedly in trouble with his military superiors, and was finally put on non-active status as a punishment for "Consorting in public with a woman of loose morals."[4] Meanwhile, his family, exasperated by his extravagant expenditures, went to court to limit his access to his inheritance.

NORTH AFRICA

News of a rebellion against the French Empire in North Africa aroused Charles's interest in returning to active duty, and he hastily asked permission to rejoin his unit and go to Algeria to take part in combat. In June 1881, he sailed from Marseille for Oran, Algeria. Once in Africa, the spoiled, bored playboy abruptly transformed into a courageous, disciplined cavalry officer who quickly became fascinated with Africa and the desert. In combat he demonstrated genuine bravery, risking his life and earning a reputation as an excellent officer. In Algeria, Charles began what has been called his "first conversion."[5] This was not a religious conversion but a quest for power and knowledge, an unbridled drive to learn all he could about this new environment. Unlike most French officers, he wanted to know the people of the land, and he began to study Arabic. He immersed himself in books about the history and geography of the Maghreb. Like Augustine of Hippo, Charles would go through more than one conversion; for both figures, the decision to seek wisdom and knowledge was an important, transformative moment.

After winning a reputation as a successful officer, Charles abruptly resigned from the French Army and resolved to do what no European had hitherto done: explore the uncharted interior and southern areas of Morocco, which was still independent from the European empires. In Algiers he made the acquaintance of an Irishman, Oscar MacCarthy, who had been a pioneering

---

4. Antier, *Charles de Foucauld*, 54.
5. Antier, *Charles de Foucauld*, 59.

explorer of southern Algeria. MacCarthy supported Charles's hopes, but he knew that Sultan Mouray Hassan of Morocco would be far away and had little control over these regions, and there would be no French Army at hand to rescue him. For safety, MacCarthy encouraged Charles to travel in the guise of a poor, wandering Jewish rabbi. MacCarthy introduced Charles to Mardochée Abi Serour, a Jewish man who had been born in southern Morocco and who became intrigued by the project and agreed to guide Charles. And so in 1883, the onetime aristocratic playboy disguised himself as a Jew and embarked with a Jewish guide on an epic and dangerous journey through the interior of Morocco, depending on Jewish hospitality, losing his money and nearly his life, but holding on to his scientific instruments and all the while compiling invaluable geographical information about areas unknown to Europeans.

Because there was considerable prejudice against Jews from both Arab Muslims and French Catholics, the assumption of a Jewish persona was an experience of humiliation that would be a harbinger of Charles's later spiritual path. But for the moment his ambitions were scholarly, not spiritual. His goal was to write a major academic study of the geographic, social, and political conditions in this region. He was moved by the beauty of the landscape, the devotion of his Jewish hosts, and by the intensity of Muslims celebrating the night of power in Ramadan.[6] After traveling for months across the Atlas Mountains and the desert, Charles presented himself to the French consulate in Tisint, unrecognizable. The secretary could hardly believe this straggly, undernourished beggar was a French viscount, but after Charles had washed and changed his appearance, he was welcomed. The French consul offered him passage on a ship departing for Marseille, but Charles insisted he would travel overland through dangerous areas on a return trip to Algeria. The French chancellor could not believe that Charles intended to travel for two to three months through dangerous territory when a ship was

---

6. Antier, *Charles de Foucauld*, 78–79.

waiting. After many months of further travel, Charles arrived in Algeria and presented himself to a French military base. Though he looked like an impoverished beggar, he presented a scrap of paper to be given to the commander: "Viscount Charles de Foucauld, Lieutenant in the African Fourth Chasseurs."[7] At first none of the officers recognized him, but he greeted one by name, and suddenly his identity was accepted, and he was celebrated as a hero.

His scientific contributions were significant. He was the first Frenchmen to cross the three Atlas mountain ranges. He had mapped 1,700 miles of previously unknown trails, as well as 3,000 elevations; and he had recorded thousands of observations. The Geographical Society of Paris recognized his scientific contributions by admitting him as a member in 1884 and by granting him its gold medal, its highest recognition of scholarly achievement, in January 1885. A few months later, the Sorbonne bestowed on him its own gold medal. Restless to learn more, he returned to Algeria for further exploration in 1885, returning to France in January 1886, which would prove to be the decisive year in his religious journey.

TRANSFORMATION IN PARIS

Charles settled into a routine of work in Paris, transforming his notes into the book that would appear in 1888, *Reconnaisance au Maroc*.[8] His old friends recognized a profound change; the young playboy who loved to party was now immersed in academic work. He detached himself from romantic relationships with women, and he read the Holy Qur'an, recalling the devotion of Muslims in the Maghreb. "Islam has produced in me a profound upheaval," he later wrote in a 1901 letter to Henri de Castries. He continued, "Observing this faith and these souls living with God as a continual presence has allowed me to glimpse

---

7. Antier, *Charles de Foucauld*, 82.

8. Charles de Foucauld, *Reconnaisance au Maroc* (reprint, Vendres, France: Editions d'Aujourdhui, 1985 [1888]).

something greater and more true than worldly occupations."[9] But he did not see Islam as a divine revelation, and he was very critical of the prophet of Islam.

Charles began reading the writings of the famous seventeenth-century preacher and bishop, Jacques-Benigne Bossuet. He was especially moved by Bossuet's challenge to form in oneself "the Holy Trinity, unity with God, knowledge of God, love for God. And since our knowledge, which for now is imperfect and obscure, will depart, and since the love in us is the sole thing that will never depart, let us love, let us love, let us love."[10] He spent significant time with his cousin Marie de Bondy, who was a very devout Catholic. This prompted him to reflect: "Since she possesses such an intelligent soul, the religion in which she so firmly believes cannot be the madness I think it."[11]

Charles would look back on this period of his life and, like Augustine of Hippo, see the hand of God at work in his life at a time when he did not recognize it. He was searching for a God who was already close to him but whom he had not recognized: "I admired and wanted virtue, but I did not know you [God]."[12] The witness of Jews and Muslims to the one God impressed and intrigued him, but he did not yet have the gift of faith in any tradition. Reading Bossuet led him to ponder the necessity of faith, but he commented, "I seek the light and I do not find it."[13]

During this time of seeking and indecision, Charles met Henri Huvelin, the curate at Saint-Augustin Church, who was already the confessor of his cousin Marie and her mother. In his preaching Huvelin affirmed that Jesus came to save the suffering and the poor: "When we wish to convert a soul, we must not preach: we must show our love"; "Only God converts."[14] Huvelin

---

9. Antier, *Charles de Foucauld*, 93.
10. Antier, *Charles de Foucauld*, 94.
11. Antier, *Charles de Foucauld*, 95
12. Antier, *Charles de Foucauld*, 97.
13. Antier, *Charles de Foucauld*, 98.
14. Antier, *Charles de Foucauld*, 99.

believed that the Eucharist was not a reward for the good but a power that could bring us to Jesus Christ.[15] On October 30, 1886, Charles went to meet Huvelin in the confessional before Mass. Charles explained that he did not intend to receive the sacrament because he did not have faith. He only wanted to learn about the Catholic religion. Huvelin instructed him to say the *Confiteor* and confess his sins. Charles did so, confessing sins from his entire life. The priest gave him absolution and asked him if he had eaten anything that day. On hearing that Charles had not eaten, Huvelin instructed him to receive Communion at the Mass that would follow. To his surprise, Charles experienced a deep sense of joy and peace, and his doubts had disappeared.

As soon as Charles came to faith in God, he knew that he would dedicate his entire life to serving God: "As soon as I came to believe there was a God, I understood that I could not do otherwise than live only for him. My religious vocation dates from the same hour as my faith."[16] He embarked on a series of experiments in carrying out this mission. Charles placed his complete trust in Huvelin, who became his most trusted spiritual guide until the death of Huvelin in 1910. By 1888 Charles had left behind his interest in geography and science and also any concern for the fortune he inherited. Because Jesus had humbled himself and taken the last place, Charles wanted to follow his example, especially the hidden life of Jesus at Nazareth when he worked in obscurity and poverty in obedience to the Father. Charles stressed the importance of Jesus's abjection, encompassing his descent, his obscurity, and his rejection. Charles plunged into reading the lives of the Desert Fathers, as well as the writings of Teresa of Avila, who would become his most influential reading after the Bible.

---

15. Antier, *Charles de Foucauld*, 103.
16. Antier, *Charles de Foucauld*, 104.

Religious Life

In the summer of 1888 his cousin Marie de Bondy took him to visit a Trappist monastery, and he was attracted to this form of religious life. In 1890 he entered the Trappist monastery of Notre-Dame-des-Neiges in the mountains of Vivarais in the southeast of France. In June 1890 he moved to the Trappist monastery at Cheiklé in Syria (not far from Aleppo), which was dependent on Notre-Dame-des-Neiges. He lived as a Trappist monk for seven years. Because of his educated background and leadership skills, his superiors wanted him to be ordained a priest and eventually to serve as novice master or in higher positions. Charles became more and more dissatisfied, seeking greater experiences of poverty and abjection. In 1897, Charles was released from his vows by the Trappists, and he dreamed of founding a new community of Little Brothers of Jesus, who would live a life of strict poverty, manual labor, prayer, and service to the poor. He sought a life of greater renunciation and obscurity than he had with the Trappists.

Traveling to Palestine, he found a place serving the Poor Clares, the poorest order of nuns in Nazareth, where Jesus spent the years of his hidden life in obscurity. He contemplated the suffering of Jesus and his concern for the poor. He began to be called Brother Charles of Jesus. In prayer he knew both moments of exaltation and oneness with God and also moments of aridity and darkness. On June 6, 1897, he wrote words that would prove to be prophetic. He imagined Jesus speaking to him: "Think that you are to die a martyr, stripped of everything, stretched out on the ground, naked, unrecognizable, covered with wounds and blood, violently and painfully killed, and do you wish that it were to happen today? Consider that your whole life is to lead you toward this death. And see thus the insignificance of so many things. Think often of this death, both to prepare yourself for it and to judge things at their true value."[17]

---

17. Antier, *Charles de Foucauld*, 157–58. See also Charles de Foucauld, *Charles de Foucauld: Writings, Selected with an Introduction by Robert Ellsberg* (Maryknoll, NY: Orbis Books, 1999), 77.

Charles sought to imitate the hidden life of Jesus in everything he did. Early in 1898 he had experiences of mystical illumination during which he merged with Christ. When he returned to the monastery of the Poor Clares in Nazareth, they remarked the light of God shining in his face and deemed him a saint.[18] The superior of the Poor Clares in Jerusalem wanted to meet him, and she hoped he would be ordained and be a chaplain to her community. He was ordained a priest of the Diocese of Vivriers on June 9, 1901; but instead of serving the Poor Clares in Palestine, he returned to Algeria to begin the final stage of his life.

MINISTRY IN ALGERIA

In Beni Abbès, Algeria, an area recently conquered by the French not far from the border with Morocco, Charles built a hermitage where he lived simply and humbly, administering sacraments to French soldiers, and offering hospitality and charity to all in the area between 1901 and 1905. In 1905 he moved further south to Tamanrasset, in the region of the Ahaggar volcanic mountains, where he was more distant from French troops and other Catholics. Here he came to know and love the Tuareg people, and he worked on a four-volume Tuareg-French dictionary, which Maria Letizia Cravetto suggests can be viewed in his case as a form of spiritual and mystical practice.[19]

Charles told his apostolic vicar, Bishop Guérin: "I am and shall remain a silent, hidden monk and not a preacher. I am too unworthy to proclaim the Gospel. I can only try to live it."[20] He did not try to convert Muslims, and he came to believe that they could receive salvation from God on the path of Islam, as he wrote to a Protestant doctor: "I am here, not to convert the Tuareg in a single stroke, but to try to understand them and improve them. I am certain the Lord will welcome in heaven

---

18. Antier, *Charles de Foucauld*, 159.
19. Maria Letizia Cravetto, "A New Mystic Practice? On Charles de Foucauld's Tuareg-French Dictionary," *Diogenes* 61, no. 1 (2016): 89–96.
20. Antier, *Charles de Foucauld*, 207.

those who led good and upright lives, without their having to be
Roman Catholics."[21] Ariana Patey describes his approach to the
people: "His missionary work was still based on his principle
of silence. He never preached to the people; instead his discussions on religion were based on meditating on commonalities
between the two faiths and on moral issues."[22] He sought to
make Christ present to the Tuareg people and to all through
his practice of silence, abjection, prayer, and service to the poor.
They responded by viewing him as a marabout, and his reputation spread throughout the surrounding area. On one occa-
sion the French general Lyautey worried about Charles traveling
alone through the desert. Captain Regnault responded: "Sir, are
you not aware that Father de Foucauld never needs an escort?
Alone on horseback, he can pass by all the *rezzou* [bands of
pillagers] without fear of rifle fire. The people he encounters on
the road will prostrate themselves, kiss the hem of his burnous,
asking for his blessing! Let him go."[23]

Charles wanted the French Empire to help spread the Gospel,
but he viewed the colonial enterprise in practice as often a cause
of shame.[24] He was very critical of many French practices that
he viewed as unjust and oppressive, but he in principle fully
embraced the French vision of a *mission civilisatrice,* bringing
the benefits of Christianity and civilization. Thus he has been
viewed as one of the French "colonial heroes"; Berny Sèbe notes
that Charles was compared to Colonel T. E. Lawrence ("Lawrence of Arabia") for his knowledge of and integration into the
indigenous people.[25] Charles had a major influence on the young

---

21. Antier, *Charles de Foucauld,* 266.
22. Ariana Patey, "Sanctity and Mission in the Life of Charles de Foucauld," *Studies in Church History* 47 (2011): 374 (365–75).
23. Antier, *Charles de Foucauld,* 226.
24. Antier, *Charles de Foucauld,* 207, 217.
25. Berny Sèbe, *Heroic Imperialists in Africa: The Promotion of British and French Colonial Heroes, 1870–1939* (Manchester, UK: Manchester
University Press, 2013), 203.

Louis Massignon, whom he hoped would join him in Algeria.[26] Massignon would later found a sodality of prayer for Muslims and would influence the young Msgr. Giovanni Battista Montini, the future Pope Paul VI.

COMMUNION IN SILENCE

One of the guiding principles of Charles's religious life was *Tibi silentium laus* ("Silence is praise to you").[27] Jesus in his hidden life in Nazareth was silent, and Charles sought to imitate this aspect of Jesus's life. In a retreat at Nazareth Charles imagined Jesus speaking to him: "Prayer is any converse between the soul and God. Hence it is that state in which the soul looks wordlessly on God, solely occupied with contemplating him, telling him with looks that it loves him, while uttering no words, even in thought."[28] In this communion of silent praise, Charles joined with his Muslim sisters and brothers in praise of the one God.

---

26. Christian S. Krokus, *The Theology of Louis Massignon: Islam, Christ, and the Church* (Washington, DC: Catholic University of America Press, 2017), 10, 14–15.
27. Foucauld, *Writings*, 50.
28. Foucauld, *Writings*, 105.

2

A Culture of Encounter— Charles de Foucauld

Little Sister Cathy Wright

In *Fratelli tutti* Pope Francis speaks about a "culture of encounter." It is an expression that he has often used. I was struck by the pope's mention of Charles de Foucauld at the end of that encyclical. He cited him as someone who tried to express this culture of encounter by his life. He wrote,

> Blessed Charles directed his ideal of total surrender to God towards an identification with the poor, abandoned in the depths of the African desert. In that setting, he expressed his desire to feel himself a brother to every human being, and asked a friend to "pray to God that I truly be the brother of all." He wanted to be, in the end, "the universal brother." Yet only by identifying with the least did he come at last to be the brother of all. May God inspire that dream in each one of us.[1]

Fratelli tutti followed upon the pope's meeting with the grand imam of Al-Azhar, Ahmad Al-Tayyeb, while on a trip to the United Arab Emirates, where on February 4, 2019, they co-signed the *Document on Human Fraternity for World Peace and Living*

---

1. Pope Francis, Encyclical Letter *Fratelli tutti* (October 3, 2020), 287.

Together. Pope Francis has shown his interest in encountering the Muslim world on many occasions, not the least of which was during his visit to Iraq in 2021 and his encounter with the supreme religious authority of many Shiite Muslims, Ayatollah Ali al-Sistani. It is not surprising that the pope would see in Br. Charles a model for such encounters, since he lived and died in the Sahara among Muslim people.

There is another quote from Pope Francis that I believe is related to this theme of encounter and which intersects with Brother Charles's "desire to feel himself a brother to every human being." In a 2016 speech to the Mexican bishops, Pope Francis speaks of "the tenderness of God as the only power capable of winning human hearts . . . of the *omnipotent weakness* of divine love . . . the irresistible force of its gentleness and the irrevocable pledge of its mercy."[2]

I am not a scholar, but I want to try to reflect on how these two concepts were expressed in Charles de Foucauld's life. They strike me as being intertwined in his life and maybe he has a little light to bring to our world and our appreciation of a culture of encounter. It is basically what Charles de Foucauld tried to express as his concept of "Nazareth." He desired to live his life in such a way that, as he wrote to his cousin, "I want all of the inhabitants—Christian, Muslim, and Jew—to see me as their brother, the universal brother."[3]

If you do a search in Wikipedia for the word "culture" you will come across the following quote by Edward S. Casey. In 1986 he wrote in part: "The very word *culture* meant 'place tilled' in Middle English, and the same word goes back to Latin *colere*, 'to inhabit, care for, till. . . . To be cultural, to have a culture, is to inhabit a place sufficiently intensely to cultivate it—to be responsible for it, to respond to it, to attend to it caringly."

---

2. Pope Francis, meeting with the bishops of Mexico, Mexico City, February 13, 2016.

3. Letter to Marie de Bondy, January 7, 1902, in Charles de Foucauld, *Lettres à Mme de Bondy* (Paris: Desclée de Brouwer, 1966), 275.

This expresses so well how culture develops over time, and
when we grow within a culture we are not even aware of what
we receive and become part of. One doesn't just breeze through
on the way to somewhere else and expect to have understood
another culture. To attend to something caringly implies having
loved it. In the Incarnation that is exactly what God did in Jesus,
the taking on of our human flesh and life. It takes more than just
nine months of gestation. It takes a life lived. It takes allowing
the soil of one's heart to be lovingly tilled, breaking up the clods
to allow space for the seed to enter and to grow and to transform the landscape of the heart. And God is the one who tills.
It's kind of like the Little Prince,[4] who learns from the fox that
it is the time wasted on watering and caring for his rose that has
made it so important.

As with us all there is an inner journey involved. Brother Charles
did not at all start out his life interested in becoming a brother to
all. He was born into a privileged class and had a tumultuous,
agnostic youth. He wandered through Morocco on a basically solo
secret geographic expedition. There God used the proximity with
the Muslim people at prayer, an encounter, to unearth within him
a need for "something greater and truer" than his own worldly
pre-occupations. I used the word unearth purposefully as an
expression of God being the one who, digging the field, discovers
a treasure. The tilling, the cultivating of the land, reveals a treasure
and it is each one of us. And God sells all in the Incarnation to
enter that field and "take possession" of it in a new way.

There would be Brother Charles's conversion, his life with
the Trappists during seven years, and then leaving the Order.
The same intuition about Nazareth and his desire to imitate
Jesus that had led him to join the Trappists eventually led him
to leave the Order. His decision was nurtured by an encounter.
He wrote, from the Trappist Monastery of Akbès, Syria where
he was living:

---

4. Antoine de Saint-Exupéry, *The Little Prince* (New York: Reynal &
Hitchcock; Paris: Gallimard, 1943).

A week ago they sent me to pray beside a poor worker, a local Catholic who had died in the neighboring hamlet. What a difference between his house and where we live. I long for Nazareth.[5]

I don't think it was purely the physical poverty of the man's house that impressed Brother Charles, although that was surely a big factor, and he spoke of his longing to share his idealized notion of the poverty of Jesus. Akbès was one of the poorest monasteries of the Order, quite dilapidated. And they had plenty of asceticism. As Charles's life was generally cloistered, it would have been unusual that he visited that man's home. What I think he was now also seeing was a life without walls, one that begged encounter by its very exposure to the "world" and, by comparison, the separation and protection from others that the monastery represented. In fact, just two years later he would be writing about the genocide of Armenian Christians throughout the area, trying to alert the international community. The local military, which was responsible for these atrocities, at the same time protected the monks who were foreign nationals. It seems to me that this is what Brother Charles grasped. It was the implications of the Incarnation, of really becoming "one with" over the course of one's life, of not being protected from life. He imagined Jesus speaking to him during a retreat in 1897:

That love: how active and alive it is, how profound, impelling Him to leap with a single bound the distance separating the finite from the infinite, using that means for our salvation, that unheard of means of the Incarnation: He, God, Creator, coming to live upon this earth. . . .[6]

---

5. Letter to Marie de Bondy, April 10, 1894, in Foucauld, *Lettres à Mme de Bondy*, 156.
6. Retraite à Ephrem (1897), in Charles de Foucauld, *Crier l'Evangile* (Paris: Nouvelle Cité, 1975), 18–19.

It's as though God could not stand the separation from us and in a single bound, the Incarnation, mingled the two "worlds." Shortly before his death, Brother Charles wrote about it like this:

> Have the greatest regard for the most humble and littlest of our brothers. . . . Let us mingle with them, be one of them. Woe to the one who, out of foolish pride, would look down on those to whom God has given the highest place. His whole life was a descent. He descended in his Incarnation, descended in becoming poor . . . in always taking the last place. He came to Nazareth, the place of the hidden life, of ordinary life, of family life which is that of most people, giving an example throughout 30 years.[7]

And this is where the second quote from Pope Francis comes in. It is the "how" of encountering the other that Brother Charles's image of the Incarnation revealed to him and that he felt impelled to *imitate*. It was the image of "the tenderness of God as the only power capable of winning human hearts . . . of the *omnipotent weakness* of divine love . . . the irresistible force of its gentleness and the irrevocable pledge of its mercy" as he told the Mexican bishops. God chose to enter our existence in total weakness. Br. Charles imagined Jesus speaking to him,

> What do I teach you through this birth? . . . In becoming such a little and gentle infant I cry out: trust! familiarity! do not be afraid of me, come to me, take me in your arms . . . do not be afraid, do not be so timid in front of such a gentle child who smiles and holds open his arms.[8]

Brother Charles had to discover what it meant to become vulnerable and to come as one who has everything to learn. As he spoke so frequently about his need to *imitate* Jesus, did he also see the gentleness and familiarity of the infant of the Incarnation

---

7. Meditation on Luke 2:8–20, June 17,1916, in Charles de Foucauld, *Lettres et carnets* (Paris: Editions du Seuil, 1958), 239.

8. Retraite à Ephrem (1897), 26.

as a model for being present to others? As God had entered his life through the gentleness and goodness of others, was he learning from the Incarnation something about how he should approach others? If it wasn't explicit, there was a process that he lived and which evolved over time, a precious one that enabled encounter to happen and transform relationships.

When he wrote the above quote he had already left the Trappists and was living a sort of hermit life in Nazareth. But this too didn't last as he felt impelled by his intuition about Nazareth. I think that in his heart he couldn't live with walls that separated him from others. He eventually was ordained and left for Beni Abbès, Algeria, where he felt his life could be the presence he dreamed of as Nazareth.

His being in Algeria was complicated because it depended to a very large extent on the French colonial/military presence and the permissions he was able to procure to live there. He was the only priest who had been given permission to live in the southern regions of the Algerian Sahara. Traveling with a military convoy for about a year throughout the Hoggar region, he got his first real taste of the Sahara and the inhabitants.

> The local people receive us well, but it is not sincere. They give in to the situation. How long will it take for them to really feel the way that they try to act? Maybe never. . . . Will they know how to distinguish between soldiers and priests, to see us as servants of God, envoys of peace, universal brothers?[9]

When he decided to settle in the Hoggar for good he had to grapple with the fact that he would not be able to say Mass or even reserve the Blessed Sacrament because of existing church regulations. Eucharist was enormously important in his life, and so this represented a true renouncement. And yet he chose to put his life at the crossroads of a different sort of encounter

---

9. Letter to Marie de Bondy, July 3, 1904, in Foucauld, *Lettres à Mme de Bondy*, 128–29.

with God, one that passed through encounters with the Tuareg people. He wrote:

> Is it better to stay in the Hoggar without being able to celebrate Holy Mass, or to celebrate and not to go? I have often asked myself the same question. Before, I would have sacrificed everything else to have the celebration of Mass. But something must be wrong with this reasoning. Ever since the time of the Apostles, the greatest saints sometimes sacrificed the possibility of this celebration in favor of spiritual works of mercy. It is good to stay here alone. Even if one isn't able to do a great deal, it is worthwhile becoming a part of the scenery; one is so approachable and so "very small."[10]

Again, the approachability and littleness in imagining his way of life. In Tamanrasset he was much more distant from the French presence. He still had some contact and even passed on to them information that he gleaned about the tribes and what was happening in his area. Yes, it was a complicated presence. He remained alone among the Tuareg and a group known as *haratins* (slaves or former slaves who were very disadvantaged). This distance from the French and immersion into another culture allowed him to slowly develop another way of seeing.

Initially he was certainly the generous and well-intentioned missionary, if a very unique sort of one. But over the years God continued to cultivate something new within him and between him and the local people. In choosing where to build his house in Tamanrasset he wrote:

> I have chosen Tamanrasset, a village of twenty campfires in the heart of the Hoggar Mountains and of the Dag Rali, the major tribe of the area, far from any sizable village. I don't think that there will ever be a military post here, nor telegraph, nor Europeans, nor mission in the

---

10. Letter to Msgr. Guérin, July 2, 1907, in Charles de Foucauld, *Correspondances Sahariennes* (Paris: Editions du Cerf, 1998), 527.

foreseeable future. I have chosen to settle in this obscure little corner, asking Jesus to bless this place where I hope to have, as my only example, his life at Nazareth.[11]

Early on, Brother Charles learned an invaluable lesson from a man by the name of Motylinski, a scholar and professor of Arabic and Berber languages in Constantine. They spent several months working together on a French-Tuareg dictionary, which he would completely rework and expand after the untimely death of Motylinski from a snake bite. When Brother Charles had arrived in Tamanrasset he had started by trying to translate the Gospels into Tamahaq, the language of the Tuareg, because he so wanted to share his treasure with them. Motylinski told him rather to listen to the life and stories of the people in order to understand and know them. Brother Charles abandoned his translation of the Gospels and worked the rest of his life on that dictionary and a collection of Tamahaq poetry and verse. The point of this work was to prepare the way for other missionaries whom he was sure would follow. What it did for him personally was to open a doorway into the lives of the people. It made room for a truer encounter. He came as one who had to learn, not to teach his own dearly loved beliefs. "To inhabit a place sufficiently intensely to cultivate it—to be responsible for it, to respond to it, to attend to it caringly."

For Brother Charles, to live in the image of Jesus of Nazareth meant reaching across the divisions of his world with nothing more than his own God-given humanity. It meant living his life so as to create bonds of understanding and respect, of breaking down barriers of hostility through simple presence. To encounter the other meant letting go in order to receive. Here, too, it was a lesson learned over time. He especially learned this during a famine that had lasted several years. He had no more reserves, having shared everything with the people. He was powerless. He then fell ill from scurvy.

---

11. Foucauld, *Lettres et carnets* (Paris: Nouvelle Cité, 1986), 48 [Tamanrasset, August 11, 1905].

I was quite ill these last days. I don't know what it is, something with the heart, I think; no cough nor chest pain. The least effort makes me so short of breath that I faint. For a day or two I thought it was the end.[12]

Now, it was the people who scrounged the area for five kilometers around in order to find him a little goat's milk to save his life. This experience of dependence and vulnerability changed everything for Charles. Was it simply their duty of hospitality according to their Muslim faith or had they learned to trust this foreigner who "spoke their language better than they"? What we know is that his relationships took a new turn after this experience. He wrote:

I spent the entire year, 1912, here in the hamlet of Tamanrasset. The company of the Tuareg is such a comfort to me. I can't tell you how good they are to me, what upright souls I have found among them. One or two are true friends—such a rare and precious thing anywhere.[13]

I think this is what Pope Francis means by a "culture of encounter." We are changed by the ones we love. They enter our hearts and mold our lives: simply living among people who are very different, of coming to know and be known by these others as brother and sister, of allowing their lives and stories to become part of the fabric of one's own life and one's own relationship with God.

Ali Merad (1930–2017), professor of Islamic studies and historian at the Sorbonne, Muslim, born in Algeria, while not claiming to speak for all of Islam, wrote about Charles de Foucauld:

Charles de Foucauld's attitude was totally different [from the Muslim marabouts of his time]. He had chosen

---

12. Letter to Marie de Bondy, July 17, 1907, in Foucauld, *Lettres à Mme de Bondy*, 166.

13. Letter to Henry de Castries, January 8, 1913, in Charles de Foucauld, *Lettres à Henry de Castries* (Bruyeres le Châtel: Nouvelle Cité, 2011), 194.

to adopt the position of the humble, the little people. . . . From his words and deeds and his enduring concern to share their difficult material conditions, they must have understood that he wished—and felt himself—to be with them simply as a man with his brothers.[14]

The foundation of Brother Charles's life and way of presence to others was his relationship with God. I believe that his encounter with God not only gave him the inner security necessary to reach out to others; it gave him an identity grounded in the knowledge that he, orphaned at the age of six, was a child of God—no matter what. That inner conviction gave him a freedom to live without walls, whether physical or psychological, to be at peace with God, himself and others, free to welcome the other without defenses. It enables trust in oneself and in the unknown other.

It calls to mind an interview of Dr. Howard Thurman, mentor to so many in the civil rights movement. He recounts how his grandmother, a former slave, always reminded him that no matter what happened in his life, that he was a child of God. She knew that he would need that knowledge in order to deal with the racism and unevenness of the world that he would encounter, of people calling him anything but a child of God. She bequeathed so much power and peace to him with those few words. It was an inner knowledge that helped him toward discovering the unity of all humankind, that in looking into the face of another he would see his own face. Rep. John Lewis recounted a similar event in his last book, *Across That Bridge*, the first chapter being "Faith." He cites it as what enabled him to welcome the man who beat him as his brother.

At the heart of Brother Charles's way of prayer was a deeply Eucharistic spirituality. He saw in the gift of Jesus's body and blood the sign of God's abiding presence among us. It is the very sign of "the tenderness of God as the only power capable of

---

14. Ali Merad, *Christian Hermit in an Islamic World* (Mahwah, NJ: Paulist Press, 1999), 74.

winning human hearts . . . of the *omnipotent weakness* of divine love . . . the irresistible force of its gentleness and the irrevocable pledge of its mercy."

The more that Brother Charles met Jesus in prayer, the more he was impelled to seek him in others. His belief in this double presence—Jesus present in the Eucharist and truly present in the other—is very important in understanding the lens through which he encountered the world and those in it.

> I believe that there are no others words of the Gospel which have made a deeper impression and transformed my life more than these: "Whatever you do to the least of these little ones, you do to me." If we imagine that these words are those of uncreated Truth and come from the mouth of him who said, "This is my body, this is my blood," with what strength are we impelled to seek and to love Jesus in these little ones, the sinners and the poor. . . .[15]

Charles de Foucauld sheds a little light on this way of encounter for our very polarized world. We can embrace the *omnipotent weakness* of the Incarnation in approaching the "other." But we must ground ourselves first in our relationship with God. We can then choose to see the other as a brother or sister.

There is nothing naïve about it. We will definitely lose something along the way and it can be costly. We may have to let go of something that we felt was essential to our way of seeing things only to discover in the costly letting go that a new way becomes apparent. That is at the heart of the Pascal Mystery. We will be gifted through this dying by rising with new eyes, new perspectives. But we have to let go in order to get there. Not easy. . . .

---

15. Jean-François Six, ed., *L'Aventure de l'amour de dieu: 80 lettres inédites de Charles de Foucauld à Louis Massignon* (Paris: Éditions du Seuil, 1993), 210.

Charles de Foucauld was transformed from a sullen and confused youth to a man of passion and joy. To say he was the "universal brother" can be a bit misleading. We love when we concretely love the one person who is before us. This is where encounter takes place.

> He was very happy living this way. It was no small thing and was clear to all. He had pushed himself to his limit, he was completely fulfilled; he was an absurdly complete human being. Maybe that was the secret of his happiness. His eyes shone with calm and silent joy.[16]

----

16. E.-F. Gautier, *L'Algérie et la métropole* (Paris: Payot, 1920).

3

Brother Charles and
the Visitation

Little Sister Kathleen of Jesus

In the silence of the desert, the grave of Brother Charles[1] bears the inscription, "I want to cry the Gospel with my whole life." Those words summarize what he wanted to live: evangelization not through words but through a way of being. He drew his inspiration from the Visitation. Mary had entered Elizabeth's house not with a speech but a simple greeting. What she carried within awoke what Elizabeth bore deep inside. Today, in a world where encounter easily becomes confrontation, this approach can help foster a fruitful fellowship between religions. Brother Charles was a precursor of the "dialogue of life."

HIS DISCOVERY OF THE MYSTERY OF THE VISITATION

Brother Charles chose the Visitation as the patron feast of the congregations he dreamed of founding. He saw it as an icon of the contemplative vocation in mission countries. When doubts about his calling as a Trappist began to surface, he gained an insight into his *special vocation* as he contemplated the Visitation. He wrote to Father Huvelin[2]:

---

1. Charles de Foucauld would sign his letters as *Brother Charles*.
2. Spiritual director who was instrumental in his conversion.

> About five and a half years ago I told you . . . that my
> dream was to imitate the Blessed Virgin in the mystery
> of the Visitation. Like her, I would silently bring Jesus
> and the exercise of the evangelical virtues, but not to the
> house of St. Elizabeth. I would go among non-Christians
> so as to sanctify them by the presence of the Blessed Sac-
> rament and the example of Christian virtues.

In the Visitation, two movements that appeared to draw
him in opposite directions came together. The first was a call
to live in silence, alone with God. The image of this was Mary
wrapped in contemplation of the One she bore within. Charles
always considered silent contemplation to be his vocation, and
it was in harmony with his temperament. The other movement
found its expression in the word *brother*, and it urged him to go
out and find Jesus in the least of his brothers and sisters. It was
illustrated by Mary setting off in haste to meet her aged cousin.
Brother Charles was often torn between what he felt to be his
vocation and what seemed to be God's will. Yet it was precisely
this tension that would lead him to sanctity.

SILENT CONTEMPLATION

When he looked back on his life, Charles realized that Jesus
Christ had visited him in his own cousin Marie de Bondy. At the
time of his conversion at 28, the strength of her testimony rested
on her way of being. "A beautiful soul reinforced your work, my
God, but by her silence, her gentleness and her goodness. She
spread her fragrant perfume. You drew me by the beauty of a
soul in whom virtue appeared so exquisite that it ravished my
heart forever."[3]

Her life spread its *perfume*. Brother Charles was fond of that
metaphor.

> Let us imitate Jesus. Let us be his instruments as Mary
> was. This mystery illustrates the duties of contemplatives

---

3. Notes from retreat in Nazareth, November 8, 1898.

towards non-Christians . . . a life that *is fragrant* with all
the evangelical virtues. O my God, I always believed that
this was what you wanted of me.[4]

Evangelii gaudium, the apostolic exhortation of Pope Francis,
recalls that "It is not by proselytizing that the Church grows
but by attraction." Gandhi's words about the gospel of the rose
come to mind. "A rose does not need to preach. It simply spreads
its fragrance. The fragrance is its own sermon."

Good perfume depends on body warmth to give off its scent.
Using imagery from the Visitation, one might say that you need
to "be pregnant" with Jesus in order to carry him to others. In
the Visitation, two pregnant women meet. Each carries a life that
doesn't belong to her, but what each one bears speaks to what is
most hidden in the other.

When he first settled in Beni Abbès, Brother Charles began
to adopt the White Fathers' style of mission. He attempted to
create a little Christian community with a few redeemed slaves
and composed a catechism for their use. But very quickly he
realized that before catechizing, he needed to create bonds with
people. An important factor, perhaps decisive in the proclama-
tion of the Gospel, was the quality of the messenger.

The good we achieve depends on what we are, not what
we do or say. It depends on the grace that accompanies our actions, the extent to which Jesus lives in us,
to which our actions are His, acting in and through us.
May this truth always be present to our minds.[5]

GOING OUT TO OTHERS

The Visitation implies silent contemplation *and* going out toward
others. During the papal conclave in March 2013, Jorge Mario
Bergoglio recalled the urgency of *going out* for the church's

---

4. Meditation on Luke 1:39–56 (1898).
5. Rule for the Association of Brothers and Sisters of the Sacred Heart,
art. XXVIII, no. 3.

mission today and he gives the example. After the annuncia-
tion Mary set off in haste, even if prudence might have dictated
otherwise. The need to announce is characteristic of Christianity.
The Samaritan woman left her jar at the well in her haste to go
tell those in her village about the one she had just encountered.
Perhaps it is only when one announces Christ that one begins to
grasp who he really is.

> What Mary undertakes in the Visitation isn't a visit to
> her cousin so that they might console and edify each
> other . . . even less is it a charitable visit to help her
> during her last few months of pregnancy and labor. It's
> so much more than that. She sets off to sanctify and
> evangelize St. John, not by words but by silently bring-
> ing him Jesus, right into his own house. The same is
> done by monks and nuns vowed to contemplation in
> mission countries.[6]

One could judge these words to be those of a man insensitive
to the difficulties related to a pregnancy late in life! But what
Brother Charles writes squares with the Gospel narrative. If the
main reason for Mary's visit to her cousin had been to help her
it would have been normal that she remain until the baby's birth.
Strangely, Luke records Mary's departure before narrating the
birth of John the Baptist. Her visit seems to have been mainly to
greet her cousin. That's where the text places the emphasis:

> She entered the house of Zechariah and *greeted* Eliza-
> beth. And when Elizabeth heard the *greeting* of Mary,
> the babe leaped in her womb; and Elizabeth was filled
> with the Holy Spirit. "For behold, when the voice of
> your *greeting* came to my ears, the babe in my womb
> leaped for joy." (Luke 1:40–44)

Mary herself had been visited by an angel who had greeted
her with the words, "Hail, full of grace, the Lord is with you!"

---

6. Meditation, Nazareth, July 2, 1898.

Immediately afterward she set off for her cousin's, urged by a Word that had taken flesh in her. Brother Charles wanted to be taken up in that same movement.

THE GREETING

As he grew in understanding of his vocation, Brother Charles began to refer to himself as a *missionary monk*, living an *apostolate of friendship*. Conversation was its privileged instrument. "I never hesitate to prolong conversations and let them last very long when I see that they are useful."[7] His goal in these conversations was to lead people to their better selves by addressing their conscience and appealing to those truths that flowed from their natural sense of religion. Love helped him discover how to go about speaking to each person.

> Let us not forget that souls are different and that, following God's example, you have to draw some people one way, others another, guide some in one manner, others in another, each according to what God has put inside of them. It would be foolishness to have only one method and want everyone to conform. You need to study people and lead them to God, each according to the way in which God calls them.[8]

He no longer approached people as a caregiver, as he did in Beni Abbès, but as a friend. His apostolate of friendship was in imitation of the One who made himself close to each human being, revealing the pleasure God takes in entering into conversation with each one.

Brother Charles left traces of his conversations with the local Tuareg chief, Moussa ag Amastane. He would prepare them carefully since you never knew when Moussa, being a nomad, would drop by. He kept a list of "Things to say to Moussa," of which the following are a few examples:

---

7. Letter to Msgr. Guérin, March 6, 1908.
8. Meditation on Psalm 51, Nazareth (1897).

- Reduce expenses. Be humble. God alone is great. He who thinks himself great, or who seeks to be great, does not know God.
- *Never lie to anybody.* All untruth is hateful to God, for God is truth.
- Never praise anyone to their face. When you think highly of someone it comes out in your actions and confidence. No use in saying it. Flattery is shameful.

He also practiced his apostolate by conversation with Christians. Dr. Hérisson recalls:

> Before sunset, Father took an hour's recreation. He used to walk up and down beside his hermitage, chatting about all kinds of things. We would walk side by side, his hand on my shoulder as he laughed and told me about the Tuaregs and some of his memories. He would begin by asking me how I had spent the day. He got me to make a sort of examination of conscience, and blamed me if I had not attended to some Tuareg, or studied their language.

What Did His Muslim Friends Think?

One might wonder what the inhabitants of the Sahara understood of the visit that God was paying them in the Christian marabout. Brother Charles often asked himself that question. After his bishop's visit to Beni Abbès he noted:

> In order to bring the Muslims to God, do you need to seek their esteem by excelling in certain things that they value? For example, by being bold, a good horseman, a lavish giver, etc. Or should you practice the Gospel in its poverty, trekking along on foot instead of mounted on a camel, doing manual work like JESUS in Nazareth? . . . The Muslims don't make a mistake. When they see a priest who's an able horseman, a good shot

they say: "He's an excellent rider, no one can shoot as
well as him." But they don't say he's a saint. Should
a missionary lead the life of St. Anthony in the desert, they will all say, "He's a saint." Natural reason will
often make them friends of the former; but when it
comes to matters regarding their souls, they will only
trust the latter.

During his trip to France with Oûksem in 1913, his Tuareg
friends wrote to him. There are about twenty of these letters,
and they allow us to sense the relationship from their point of
view.

It's me Chikat who says: warm greetings to my compan-
ion the marabout.
It's me Choumekki who says: warm greetings to the
marabout and his sister.
Everyone is well. We have no news (of you).
It's me Oûksem who says, warm greetings to the mar-
about.
It's me Abahag who says, warm greetings to the mar-
about.
It's me Litni the kalipha who says, warm greetings to the
marabout.
It's me Aflan who says, warm greetings to my father the
marabout.
It's me Abdelqadir who says, I send a lot of greetings to
the marabout.
It's me Adhan who says, warm greetings to the marabout.
It's me Adhan who says, warm greetings to Oûksem.
It's me Oûksem who says, warm greetings to my name-
sake.
It's me Adhan who says: Mokhammed ag Chikat had a
son. He still doesn't have a name.

This shower of greetings recalls the Visitation. How much benev-
olence is packed into those few words!

Evangelized by the Muslims

Mary was changed by the Visitation. The recognition by Elizabeth of what she carried within changed the young girl from Nazareth into the woman who proclaims the Magnificat. Brother Charles was also changed through his life with his *Muslim parishioners*. True encounters always sharpen our own sense of identity.

Shortly after his arrival in Tamanrasset, Brother Charles wrote to his cousin: "Having little warm clothing, the Tuareg do not go out much during the winter. Besides, they're not in much of a hurry to visit me. The ice needs to be broken." Six years later he wrote to a friend: "The Tuareg are very consoling company. I cannot express how good they are for me, how many upright souls I find among them; one or two of them are real friends, something that is everywhere so rare and so precious."[9] One of these friends was called Abahag. In another letter Brother Charles commented, "How did they become my friends? In the same way that we make bonds among ourselves. I don't give them any presents; but they came to understand me as their friend, that I was true and could be trusted. And they have reciprocated the same attitude toward me."[10]

In general, Brother Charles wrote his daily diary with telegraphic succinctness, but on learning of Abahag's illness, he became more detailed. "October 23, 1914—Found out tonight that Abahag has been unconscious since last evening. He suddenly developed very high, malarial fever. He had had a bit of fever earlier but it didn't seem very serious." The next day he noted, "October 24, 1914. Abahag died today around 4 in the afternoon. He was buried at 6pm. Took part in the burial."

That very evening, he took the sealed envelope containing his own last will and testament and wrote on the back: "I wish to be buried where I die, a simple burial, no coffin, very simple

---

9. Letter to Henry de Castries, January 8, 1913.
10. Letter to Brigadier Garnier, February 23, 1913.

grave, no monument, just a wooden cross. October 24, 1914."
Abahag's burial seems to have helped him define how he wanted
to live and die.

THE JOY OF THE VISITATION

The story of the Visitation is suffused with joy. Those who knew
Brother Charles often commented on his joy. When Dr. Hérisson
asked him for advice on how to approach the Tuareg, Charles
replied:

> Be human, charitable, *and always joyful.* You must
> always laugh, even in saying the simplest things. I, as
> you see, am always laughing, showing my ugly teeth.
> Laughter sets the other person at ease. It draws people
> closer together, allowing them to understand each other
> better. It can brighten up a gloomy character, it is a char-
> ity.[11]

Where did that joy come from? Certainly, it flowed from his
life in God, but surely it also came to him from the "very consoling company" he kept with his Tuareg friends. Brother Charles
reminds us that the church rediscovers her joy and youth when
she crosses the institutional threshold and goes out to meet the
men and women of our world.

---

11. René Bazin, *Charles de Foucauld: Hermit and Explorer* (New York:
Benzinger, 1923), 285.

4

A Life in Dialogue

Marc Hayet

Charles de Foucauld himself recounted how he came back to his childhood faith, and how this return was an encounter with Jesus of Nazareth, rediscovered as a close living friend, with a deep desire to "*breathe only for Him,*" as he likes to repeat. To a friend, he explains, "*I have lost my heart to this JESUS of Nazareth crucified 1900 years ago and I spend my life seeking to imitate him as closely as I can, in all my weakness.*"[1]

But what is remarkable about his journey is that, always in the name of the imitation of Jesus of Nazareth, he will go from a life of radical separation from the world (as a monk behind cloistered walls and as a hermit in a garden shed) to a life integrated in a milieu very different from his own—the Tuaregs of Algeria—in which he allows himself to be welcomed by the people. When Charles arrives in Algeria at the end of 1901, he comes with the desire to meet others, to encounter the one who is furthest, the most different. Of these last years of his life, we can say that he lived them "in dialogue."

Curiously, the word "dialogue" is absent from the vocabulary of Charles de Foucauld; we never come across it in the many writings and letters he left us! But, while he doesn't possess the word, he possesses the practice. He himself alludes to this when, for example, he writes to the apostolic prefect

---

1. Letter to Gabriel Tourdes, March 7, 1902.

of the Sahara, *"Living alone in a place is a good thing. You
achieve something even if you don't do much, because you start
to belong to the country. You're approachable and unimposing
there: it gives you such littleness!"*[2] Belonging "to the country,"
little and approachable, involves making an effort to erase the
distances that prevent communication. A few months before his
death, he gives a sort of rereading of his life. In search of a priest
who could take charge of the Confraternity that he would like
to create, he writes: *"I consider myself less capable of tack-
ling this enterprise than almost any other priest, having learned
only how to pray in solitude, keep silence, live with books, and
at most, chat intimately one-on-one with poor people"*[3]—a
magnificent intuition of that which he probably succeeded in
the most, learning to *"chat intimately one-on-one with poor
people"*; this can be learned! And God knows the number of
hours that Charles de Foucauld spent decoding the language,
culture, customs, and family structures of the Tuaregs whom he
asked for hospitality.

It might be useful to remember in this introduction that, pas-
sionate for Jesus of Nazareth, as we have mentioned, Charles
de Foucauld also burns with the desire to make known the one
who gives him life: "Light a fire on the earth" is the phrase of the
Gospel that he chose to write on the souvenir card of his priestly
ordination. His most beautiful intuitions on dialogue can be sit-
uated in the context of making known the Gospel that burns in
him to *"the brothers of Jesus who don't know him."*[4] We mustn't
forget either the ecclesiastical or theological context of his time;
the doctrine of "No salvation outside the church" was the background common to all Christians and missionaries.

Even if Charles de Foucauld didn't spell out a theory of dialogue, we can nonetheless recognize in his writings elements that
show how he conceived of it.

---

2. Letter to Msgr. Guérin, July 2, 1907.
3. Letter to Father Voillard, June 11, 1916.
4. Notes from the retreat before his priestly ordination (June 1901).

BANISH THE MILITANT SPIRIT

Banish far from us the militant spirit. "I send you like sheep amongst wolves," says JESUS. . . . What a big difference between the way Jesus acts and speaks and the militant spirit of those who are not Christian or who are bad Christians and who see enemies to be combated, instead of seeing sick brothers who must be cared for; wounded people lying in the road for whom we must be good Samaritans. . . . Not being militant with anyone: JESUS taught us to go "like sheep amongst wolves," not to speak bitterly, harshly or insultingly or to take up arms.[5]

"Banish the militant spirit"—today we would say "refuse all proselytism." This means refusing to convince others at all costs, refusing to place ourselves on the level of a battle of hotly defended ideas ("bitterly, harshly or insultingly or to take up arms"); this means trying to understand others, what the obstacles to dialogue are within them, what makes them "sick . . . wounded," as Brother Charles says.

RECOGNIZING THE OTHER'S VALUE, THEIR PART OF TRUTH

Islam is very seductive. It seduced me greatly. But the Catholic faith is true. It's easy to prove and consequently all the others are false. . . . Well, where there is error there is always harm (even if the truths that exist amongst the errors are good, and are always capable of producing great and true good, which is the case for Islam).[6]

Marked, as we have said, by the ideas of his time (expressed very clearly in the first part of this text!), it is given to him to see further and to open up a space that enlarges the horizon:

---

5. Letter to Joseph Hours, May 3, 1912.
6. Letter to Henri de Castries, July 15, 1901.

recognizing the other person as a bearer of the truth; recognizing that this truth is good in itself, and that, consequently, it is normal that the person we are speaking to be attached to it with the keys that he disposes of to interpret it; recognizing that this good is called to bear fruit and fruit in truth.

It's quite interesting to see that at the end of his life, Charles de Foucauld often insisted on this attitude of trust we must have in the work of truth in the heart of each person, a great trust in the uprightness of people: every human being is capable of discerning what is good, desiring it, and conforming their lives to it. In his final years, Charles worked very hard to establish an association open to all Christians (priests, lay people, single people, married people, religious brothers and sisters) that would have a triple goal: (1) placing the Gospel at the center of one's life and living from it; (2) loving the Eucharist, the sacrament of life freely given, and living from it; (3) working to make the Gospel known to those who are far from it. And he writes a sort of Rule of Life for the members of this union, the *Directory*. It is striking to observe his insistence on the idea that, before any speech, Christians put into practice the great dimensions of life: love, respect of others, sobriety of life, etc. These great values can speak to the intelligence and the heart of all: each person, in discovering the fruit that they bear when they are lived, might desire to immerse themselves in these values and put them into practice.

The fundamental attitude of dialogue: believing that the other person is sincere and sincerely seeks with the light that they dispose of, not doubting their good faith, not doubting their capacity to be open. Thus begins a path traveled together on which each person can be enriched by the values of the other person.

ENTERING A RELATIONSHIP OF RECIPROCITY: THE STORY OF TARICHAT

During the massacre at the Flatters mission, a Tuareg woman from a noble family had a very beautiful atti-

tude, she opposed herself to the killing of the wounded, took them in and nursed them in her home, refusing entrance to Attissi, who . . . wanted to finish them off himself, and after their recovery, had them repatriated to Tripoli. She is now between 40 and 43 years old, has a great deal of influence and is renowned for her charity.

Is this soul not ready for the Gospel? Would it not be called for to write to her simply to tell her that the charity she never tires of practicing and with which she took in, nursed, defended, and repatriated the wounded from the French mission, 22 years ago, is known to us and fills us with joy and gratitude to God. . . . God said, "The 1st religious commandment is to love God with all your heart. The 2nd is to love all people, without exception, as yourself." God also said, "You are all brothers. You all have the same Father, God"; and "The good and the bad that you do to others, you do to God." Admiring and thanking God to see you practicing charity toward people, which is the second obligation, the first being love of God, we write this letter to tell you that among Christians (all those who) hear about you, will bless you, praise God for your virtues, and will pray to Him to fill you with grace in this world and glory in heaven. . . . We also write to you to insist that you pray for us, certain that God, who has placed such a firm desire to love and serve in your heart, listens to the prayers that you address to Him, we ask you to pray for us and for all people, that we may love and obey Him with all our soul. To Him be glory, blessing, honour, praise, now and forever. Amen."[7]

We find here the deep motivation of Charles de Foucauld: on hearing of this woman's attitude, he would like to get in touch with her to announce the Gospel, from which, in his eyes, she already lives. But how does he go about this? First, by expressing

---

7. Journal entry at Beni Abbès, June 21, 1903.

himself in a manner comprehensible to her: Charles starts his
projected letter with two quotations from sacred texts and closes
with a formula praising God; this is a concrete way of entering
the cultural universe familiar to a believing Muslim, in order to
facilitate the exchange.

Then Charles expresses to his interlocutor the good that he
sees in her and how much he values this good; second fundamental attitude of dialogue.

But what is even more remarkable—if we remember the ecclesiastical context of the time, more than a hundred years ago—is
the fact that, as a Catholic priest, he asks a Muslim woman to
pray for him and for all people while expressing the certainty
that God will answer her prayer, given the manner in which she
practices love for her neighbor. This is not relativism: it is, for
Charles de Foucauld, a reflection of the Catholic tradition at its
deepest, recognizing that our diverse paths of faith can be mea-
sured by the quality of our service to the weakest. And that, on
this path, we can learn and receive from the other person.[8]

We have confirmation of this reciprocal giving and exchanging in the very writings of Charles: he spent a great deal of time
talking with people, especially in Beni-Abbès and Tamanrasset;
he held some real friendships with a few, friendships made of
trust and reciprocal service, exchanges of advice:

> I have at least four "friends" here on whom I can count
> completely. How did they become my friends? In the
> same way that we form bonds among ourselves. I didn't
> give them any presents; but they understood that they
> had a friend in me, that I was devoted to them, that they
> could trust me, and they have reciprocated the same atti-
> tude toward me.... There are others whom I like, whom
> I hold in high esteem, on whom I can count for many
> things. But these four, I can ask for any sort of advice,

8. Charles de Foucauld talks about all of this in his own context, but
these elements of dialogue are, of course, applicable to any everyday situation in which we find ourselves.

information or service and be sure that they will give of their best to me.[9]

We mustn't forget that when he was very sick in the winter of 1907–1908, it was the Tuaregs who took care of him and saved his life; he will remain very grateful to them.

LISTENING TO THE "LANGUAGE" OF THE OTHER PERSON: ALLOWING ONESELF TO BE TOUCHED BY LIFE

It is not our goal to talk about the enormous scientific contribution made by Charles de Foucauld to the understanding of the Tuareg language—a contribution that serves as a reference to this day—except to remind ourselves of the number of hours that Charles spent in dialogue with people in order to listen to, understand, and enter into the richness of a culture through its poems, proverbs, social organization, etc.

Over and above this work on the language, there is also an attention to the life of people around him, their feelings, their being: life is a language that one must learn to listen to. This is a constant on the journey of Charles de Foucauld: allowing himself to be questioned by what he perceives of the life of the world around him, to the point of changing direction thanks to these silent interrogations. Entering into dialogue is accepting the risk that the life of another person questions and changes me.

We already find this during his journey to Morocco:

Islam made a very deep impression on me. The sight of such faith, of people living continually in the presence of God, gave me an insight into something greater and truer than worldly pursuits: "ad majora nati sumus"[10] *. . . I started studying Islam, then the Bible, and by the*

---

9. Letter to Brigadier Garnier, February 23, 1913.
10. "We are born for greater things."

action of God's grace, my childhood faith found itself affirmed and renewed. . . .[11]

When he is a Trappist, it is also the situation of the people around him that questions and destabilizes him and transforms his dreams:

Eight days ago, I was sent to attend the wake of a poor local Catholic who had died in the next village: what a difference between his house and our buildings. I long for Nazareth. . . .[12]

Our biggest job is the work in the fields: . . . The day before yesterday we finished the harvest. It is the work of peasants, work that is infinitely good for the soul: while occupying the body, it leaves time for the soul to pray and meditate. And this work, more difficult than one would think if one had never done it, imparts such compassion for the poor, such charity for workers, for laborers! One realizes the price of a piece of bread when one sees for oneself how much suffering it costs to produce![13]

Later, in Nazareth, it is also when he realizes that he himself is well treated while other visitors to the monastery are less so that he experiences a certain discomfort and begins to think about leaving:

The Mother Abbess is always so good to me, so good that she is always inventing new ways of being kind to me; and the whole community does the same. . . . But this in itself bothers me; and this is why: I don't want to be ungrateful; but I don't want to fall into flattery, which is just as undignified; however, if the Reverend Mother has this extreme goodness towards me, . . . this doesn't

---

11. Letter to Henri de Castries, July 8, 1901.
12. Letter to Marie de Bondy, April 10, 1894.
13. Letter to Mimi, his sister, July 3, 1891.

*prevent her from being quite hard, quite cold and harsh
on others who are better than me and who, in any case,
are all members of Jesus. . . . . There is sometimes an
absence of charity, or even justice which puts me in a
difficult situation, even more so because nobody dares
mention it to me—people know, or guess what I would
say about it—and everybody tries to hide these things
from me. One should be frank and honest by explain-
ing things frankly: but I cannot do so without causing
problems for those who come to me with their suffering,
. . . and thus, not to fall into flattery, or be complicit, or
in any way participant in this manner of doing things,
I've thought more than once about leaving and taking
advantage of this departure to go to a place in which I
am truly, and remain, absolutely unknown.*[14]

It is interesting, in this last citation, to note that, as much
of a hermit as he is in his garden shed, he is in contact with
people and listens to them attentively enough to receive their
confidences and the expression of their suffering: this listening
to the lives of others shakes him and questions him to the point
of envisaging a change of direction.

And we might suppose that it was because he knew his friend
and his capacity to allow life to question him that Laperinne
wrote Charles the account of the charity of Tarichat: a way of
peaking his interest in making contact with the Tuaregs, which
will eventually lead him to settle in Tamanrasset.

Perhaps we can conclude this rapid overview of the way in
which Charles de Foucauld envisages dialogue by taking a look
at what is, no doubt, the key to understanding his attitude. In
the letter that we quoted at the beginning, in which Charles
advises to "banish the militant spirit," he clearly expresses that
to him, there is only one way of entering into a true relationship
with someone: it is *"through goodness, tenderness, fraternal*

---

14. Letter to Father Huvelin, March 22, 1900.

affection, the example of virtue, by humility and gentleness which are always attractive and so very Christian." He will insist, throughout his life, on this dimension of tenderness which opens doors: "*Have that tender kindness which enters into the details and knows, through little nothings, how to put balm on people's hearts.*"[15] And he summarizes all of this in a deep and simple formula which he underlines himself, "*Above all, see in each human being, a brother.*"[16] To live in dialogue is to see all those whom I encounter as brothers and sisters, and act toward them in such a way that they themselves can "*look on me as their brother, the universal brother!*"[17] For the key to dialogue is always in the other person's hand: I can hold out my hand, it is always the other person who might seize it and say to me, "Come in, you are my brother!"

15. Meditation on the Gospel of Mark 5:35–43, the resurrection of Jairus's daughter
16. Letter to Joseph Hours, May 3, 1912.
17. Letter to Marie de Bondy, January 7, 1902.

5

From the Sacrament of the Altar
to the Sacrament of Brother

Msgr. Claude Rault, MAfr (Père Blanc)

I want all the inhabitants to get used to looking upon me as their brother, a universal brother.

Declared Blessed in November 2005, by Pope Benedict XVI, St. Charles de Foucauld, who has often been called "the hermit of the desert," was canonized by Pope Francis on May 15, 2022. This was an event of significance not only for the Catholic Church of North Africa but also for the universal church, on account of the wide influence of the spirituality of Charles de Foucauld and the numerous branches of the spiritual family that are related to him. These branches have now spread throughout the whole world. The life of this saint is marked by a rather unexpected conversion, since he had lost the faith, and by his desire to imitate Jesus of Nazareth, a desire that would lead him to the extreme south of the Algerian desert.

A YOUTH MARKED BY THE LOSS OF THE FAITH

Born on September 15, 1858, in Strasbourg, France, in a well-to-do family, by the time he was six years old Charles had lost both his father and his mother. This loss in his infancy was to cause an emotional wound that would mark his whole life. He was entrusted to the care of his grandfather. He gave himself over to study, but this was the beginning of a life of torment. During his studies, feeding himself on books that suited his attraction for an easy life without God, he lost the faith.

At the age of 20, he embarked on a military career, entering the military academy of St. Cyr and then going on to the school for cavalry in Saumur where he managed to graduate—finishing the last of his year. He was living an unregulated life, full of good meals and good company. He formed an attachment with a loose-living woman, but then his regiment was posted to Algeria. He left for Algeria with this woman, and since he refused to be separated from her, he was dismissed from the army for misconduct. He returned to France with her and took up lodging in a luxury hotel near the Swiss border. Not long afterward, however, on learning that his regiment was going into action, he abandoned his lady friend and returned to Algeria, where he was reincorporated into the army for the military expedition.

He found this life of adventure in the open air attractive, and his way of life began to change. Together with his fellow soldiers, he got the taste of an active life, simple, even Spartan—but it ended with a return to barracks that was hardly to his liking. At age 23, he opted for a definitive return to civilian life. Craving adventure, between 1882 and 1884 he prepared and carried out a dangerous journey of exploration in Morocco. This was a great success, but this did not satisfy him. He was now 26 years old.

Having returned to France, his search for another adventure that would give meaning to his life was his main preoccupation and filled his thoughts. He would go from church to church making what he himself called "a strange prayer": "*My God, if you exist, then let me know you.*" In Morocco and in Algeria he had been struck by the Muslims he had met. He wrote later: "*Islam produced in me a profound upheaval. The sight of this faith, of people living in the continual presence of God, gave me a glimpse of something greater and more real than worldly occupations."*

HIS CONVERSION AND THE SEARCH FOR A LIFE GIVEN TO GOD

Following the advice of his cousin Marie de Bondy, at the end of October 1886—he had now reached the age of 28—Charles went to the Church of St. Augustine in Paris and met with Father Huvelin, a well-known priest, who invited him on the spot to make his confession and to receive Communion. This marked a new departure for Charles. His conversion brought him to give his life totally to the Lord. He would write: *"As soon as I came to believe that there was a God, I understood that I could not do otherwise than to live only for Him."* It remained for him, however, with the help of Huvelin who had become his spiritual director to see how he was to consecrate his life to God. First of all he paid a visit to Nazareth, where the poverty of the place made a great impression on him. Then he visited different monasteries and made a retreat with the Jesuits in Clamart near Paris. In agreement with Huvelin he opted for the monastic life.

After seven years of searching in the contemplative way (a few months at the Cistercian Abbey of Notre-Dame-des-Neiges in France, and then six years in the monastery of Akbès in Syria), he decided to give up the monastic life and returned to Nazareth, taking employment as a handyman at the convent of the Poor Clares (1897). He was now 38. There he divided his time between manual work, long hours of adoration before the Blessed Sacrament, and meditation on the Scriptures. It was there, in Nazareth, that his real vocation came to maturity: to live like Jesus of Nazareth. But he discovered that this treasure that he carried in himself could not be kept to himself; he had to share it. This he would do through becoming a priest, something that he had always set aside. He returned to France, and, after a year of preparation, he was ordained a priest on June 9, 1901, in Viviers Diocese.

LIFE IN THE DESERT:
LIKE JESUS OF NAZARETH

He requested of the bishop of Viviers permission to leave for the Sahara and, with the agreement of the bishop of this region, he left for Beni Abbès, a small village in the south of Algeria. There he built a hermitage with the hope of attracting some companions. He would remain there five years with this wish: "*I want all the inhabitants to get used to looking upon me as their brother, a universal brother.*"

In August 1905, when he was 47 years old, wishing always to be among "the farthest away," and at the invitation of his friend Laperrine, a French soldier who was in command of the region, he settled in Tamanrasset. He became the friend of the Amenokal, the local Tuareg chief. He led there an existence torn in different directions: prayer, study, traveling, contacts with the Tuaregs, whose language he set himself to learn with passion, and relations—somewhat difficult at times—with the French soldiers present in the region. He was sharing the life of the people, close to all, whether slaves or noble Tuaregs. In 1908, in the midst of a drought that had hit the area (there had been no rain for two years), he fell ill with scurvy. He had given all his provisions to the starving population, and he was preparing to die. Being alone, he could no longer celebrate Mass. He was near death and despair. It was his Tuareg friends who saved his life, giving him milk from the skinny goats, milk usually reserved for the children. He who had always been eager to give received his own life from his friends and neighbors.

His equanimity was grounded in a deep relationship with his *Beloved Brother and Lord Jesus*, and in an equally deep friendship with the local population. His joy was to be able to celebrate Mass alone, permission for this having arrived from the Holy Father shortly after his return to health. He was working intensely: he transcribed six thousand lines of Tuareg poetry and composed a dictionary of the Tuareg language in four volumes! War broke out between France and the Axis of Germany and

Italy. He would have liked to return to France as a chaplain and male nurse, but his friends advised him to remain in Tamanrasset. He arranged for the construction of a *borj* (a fortified residence) as a shelter for the inhabitants of the village and went to live there himself.

With the support of Italy, Tuareg tribes (the Senoussiya) from Libya began raiding in the south of the Sahara. They wanted to take the "Christian marabout" prisoner. The evening of December 1, 1916, they arrived at the *borj*. They managed to trick him into opening the door. He was dragged outside, bound hand and foot, and left under the guard of a young Tuareg. Then two camel drivers in the service of the French army arrived; the young Tuareg took fright and shot the marabout in the head. Charles collapsed and gave up his life to God. He had foreseen and almost desired this death, having meditated on this passage from the Gospel of John: *"Unless a wheat grain falls on the ground and dies, it remains only a single grain; but if it dies, it yields a rich harvest"* (John 12:24). He was buried in the shadow of his *borj*. Sometime later, an officer, detailed to clear up the belongings of Brother Charles, which had been left in disarray, found in the sand the little monstrance with the Blessed Sacrament—a sign of the gift of his life in the manner of his Lord and Master.

THE HERITAGE OF
CHARLES DE FOUCAULD FOR TODAY?

There is first of all his conversion, almost sudden, radical. Searching for meaning, during his stays in Morocco and Algeria, he had observed many Muslims praying to the One God; this had left him wondering for a long time. It is wonderful to see that God made use of Muslims to allow Charles to grasp that faith in him can give meaning to life. This first awakening brought Charles back to the faith of his childhood, but this faith would become centered more and more on Jesus, and on Jesus "in" Nazareth. It is important to mention Jesus in Nazareth, because this is the

way Charles wanted to live, after the manner of the Man from
Galilee, in the humble house of this village in Galilee. He wrote
to one of his friends: "*Love cannot be separated from imitation.
The one who loves wants to imitate: this is the secret of my life.
I lost my heart to this Jesus of Nazareth and I have spent my life
trying to imitate him.*" He wrote again: "*I didn't want to imitate
his public life and his preaching: so I had to imitate the hidden
life of the humble workman at Nazareth.*"

He was deeply motivated to go to as remote a place as possible in order to live this ideal. This is what pushed him toward
the Sahara; his concern in going there was not to live as a hermit, nor for preaching, but in order to meet the poorest of the
poor and to take among them the last place . . . a place already
occupied, as Father Huvelin wrote to Marie de Bondy, Charles's
cousin: "*Jesus took the lowest place so utterly that no one has
ever been able to get it away from him.*"

As a person of faith, and as a sage, through his concern for
incarnation, Charles engaged respectfully in the study of the
language and culture of the Muslims. His vocation, in his own
words, was "*to cry out the Gospel by the whole of my life*"
rather than to proclaim it from the rooftops. This is what distin-
guished him from the missionaries of his time. How to fulfill this
vocation? He would have much preferred manual work, closer
to the imitation of Jesus of Nazareth. So he wrote to Huvelin,
his spiritual director: "*Should the hours dedicated to work be
used entirely for manual work in the garden, or for the study
of the Tuareg language, or a part of the time for the one and
another part for the other. My inclination is for the latter . . . for
the present to give the principal part to the production of a dictionary and a grammar of the Tuareg language and the Tuareg
translation of some parts of the Scriptures. . . .*" So he worked
long days on Tuareg poetry (six thousand lines transcribed and
deciphered), and he left behind a dictionary of Tuareg in four
volumes that still today enjoys authority among linguists.

This way of proceeding is important for a proper understanding of mission, even today; it anticipates the task of inculturation,

encouraged by the Second Vatican Council that is incumbent on every worker in the vineyard of the Gospel who wishes to give witness to Jesus. This remains urgent today, even as regards the understanding of our modern world, which is not without evangelical values.

The Eucharist remained at the center of the life and being of Brother Charles. This was his motivation for being ordained a priest. After arriving in Beni Abbès, where he first settled, he wrote to one of his friends: "*Priest since last June, I have felt called immediately to go to the 'lost sheep,' to the souls that are most abandoned, the most neglected.*" To another correspondent, a few years later, he wrote: "*This divine banquet, of which I became the minister, had to be offered not to brothers, to relatives, to rich neighbors, but to the lame and the blind, to the poorest, to the souls that are most abandoned lacking priests the most.*" He lived from the Eucharist, through adoration and through its celebration . . . even if sometimes he was deprived of this.

The passion for Christ in the Eucharist went together with the "Sacrament of the Brother." At the end of his life Charles wrote to one of his friends: "*There is not, I believe, any word of the Gospel that has made a deeper impression on me and worked a greater transformation in my life than this one: 'All that you do for one of these little ones, it is for me that you do it.' When one bears in mind that these are the words of Uncreated Truth, from the same lips that said: 'this is my Body . . . this is my Blood,' how compellingly one is led to seek and to love Jesus in 'these little ones,' these sinners, these poor people, using all material means to alleviate their earthly suffering.*"

So the love of the littlest ones impels Charles to meet Jesus in the poor person and the other who is different. In the times in which we live, is it not urgent to maintain the link between the celebration of the Eucharist and the service of the poorest?

The spiritual posterity of Charles de Foucauld continues to spread, through vocations dedicated to the "life of Nazareth." Everywhere in the world there are groups of religious, women

and men, of priests, of lay people, who are living according to
the spirit of Nazareth.

The "spiritual family of Charles de Foucauld" has several
thousand members, men and women, belonging to twenty different branches. Some are more intent on the contemplative life,
even the monastic life; others opt for an evangelical presence in
the world; still others have a more apostolic orientation.

Charles de Foucauld, through lights and shadows, has opened
up for us the meaning of universal brotherhood. To recognize
this dimension of life according to the Gospel is urgent for
our church. It runs the danger, in the difficult times in which
we are living, of turning in on itself, of remaining enclosed in
the "upper room." Charles de Foucauld spent his life building
bridges toward those who are the furthest away, the poorest, the
most abandoned. He looked upon Muslims as his brothers. He
invites us to go out of ourselves, following the way traced out by
Jesus, the way of universal brotherhood to gather into unity the
scattered children of God.

6

"God Gave the Growth": A Legacy of Charles de Foucauld

Bonnie Bowman Thurston

Pope Francis's encyclical *Fratelli tutti* closes with reference to Blessed Charles de Foucauld, whose mission in the Moroccan deserts apparently had such meager effect in his lifetime. Yet Brother Charles endures as a sterling example not just of inter-religious dialogue but of familial respect for those different from one's self and culture. "Only by identifying with the least," Pope Francis writes, "did he come at last to be the brother of all."[1]

Foucauld reminds us of two fascinating things about the formation and recognition of saints. First, their early lives often are quite unsaintly (as Foucauld's biography attests). Second, the processes of holiness seem to operate by no recognizably human time table. (The cause for Foucauld's beatification began in 1927.) Like our Lord's, a saint's life may end in apparent failure, but, like the mustard seed in his parable, a great tree may spring from it. As St. Paul explained, one plants, another waters, "but only God . . . gives the growth" (1 Corinthians 3:6–7). God grew Brother Charles's good seed. Two of its vigorous "plants" are religious communities springing from Foucauld's charism and a critically important "vine" of Muslim-Christian dialogue.

---

1. Quoted in Christopher Lamb, "A better way is possible," *The Tablet,* October 10, 2020 (274/9372), 5.

Many have, do, and will shelter under the tree of congregations founded through Foucauld's influence, notably the Little Brothers of Jesus, founded in the Sahara in 1933 by René Voillaume and four companions as Petits Frères du Sacré-Coeur,[2] and the Little Sisters of Jesus, Petites Soeurs de Jésus, founded in Algeria in 1936 by Sr. Magdeleine.[3] Spiritual children of Foucauld continue to flourish in these orders, those they serve, and in international religious and lay fraternities.[4]

Also directly from seed Brother Charles planted in the sandy soil of Muslim Morocco, an important Muslim-Christian dialogue flowered in the twentieth century. Foucauld was a formative influence on French academic and spiritual master Louis Massignon, who influenced Thomas Merton, OCSO, arguably American's most famous monastic spiritual writer and an important voice in inter-religious dialogue (especially with Buddhism and Islam). Merton's correspondence with the Pakistani Muslim Abdul Aziz is one of the most complete Muslim-Christian dialogues from the mid-twentieth century. An outline of the "family tree" of dialogue that grew directly from Foucauld's "root" follows.[5]

---

2. See René Voillaume, *Brothers of Men: Letters to the Petits Frères* (London: Darton, Longman & Todd) 1966.

3. See Kathryn Spink, *The Call of the Desert: A Biography of Little Sister Magdeleine of Jesus* (London: Darton, Longman & Todd, 1993). At her death in 1991 there were 1,400 Little Sisters from 60 nationalities.

4. For more, see appendices in Jean-Jacques Antier, *Charles de Foucauld (Charles of Jesus)* (trans. Julia Shirek Smith; San Francisco: Ignatius Press, 1999) 329–34.

5. This section relies on essays by an eminent scholar at the Catholic University of America, Sidney H. Griffith, S.T., "Merton, Massignon, and the Challenge of Islam," and Griffith, "'As One Spiritual Man to Another': The Merton-Abdul Aziz Correspondence," in Rob Baker and Gray Henry, eds., *Merton and Sufism: The Untold Story* (Louisville, KY: Fons Vitae, 1999). My professional and personal debts to him are considerable.

FOUCAULD AND LOUIS MASSIGNON

Born in Paris in 1883, Massignon became one of France's most important, influential Islamic scholars and the world's great orientalists. Raised Roman Catholic by his mother, like Foucauld, Massignon traveled to North Africa (1903) to work on his thesis. After mastering Arabic, Massignon studied in Cairo (1906), where he encountered the writings of Muslim mystic al-Hallaj (858–922) who became the subject of his doctoral dissertation. That work, *La Passion d'al Husayn ibn Mansour al-Hallaj* (2 vols.; Paris: Geuthner, 1922), largely initiated study of Sufism and Islamic mysticism in the West.[6]

Massignon's subsequent development and spiritual biography are fascinating. It is tempting to describe his marriage (1914), priesthood in the Melkite Rite (1950), and the development of a sodality, *al-Badaliyyah*[7] (root *badal*), derived from al-Hallaj and based on the practice of mystical substitution, taking on another's suffering, the "substitution of one person and his merits and prayers for the salvation of someone else."[8] Widely published on many topics,[9] Massignon was an active participant in France's Catholic renaissance (which included such figures as J. K. Huysmans, Pierre Teilhard de Chardin, Gabriel Marcel, Georges Bernanos, François Mauriac, and Jacques Maritain). Professor Griffith describes him as "that rarity in the modern world, a

---

6. Massignon's work has been translated from the French by Herbert Mason and is available in the Bollingen Series of Princeton University Press. And see the entry on al-Hallaj in *Early Islamic Mysticism* (ed. and trans. Michael A. Sells; New York: Paulist Press, 1996).

7. Pope Paul VI belonged to the sodality. The movement based in Cairo under the name *Dar as-Salam* (House of Peace) published several periodicals, copies of which Massignon arranged to have sent to Merton.

8. Griffith, "Merton, Massignon, and the Challenge of Islam," 55.

9. See Jean-Jacques Waardenburb, "L. Massignon's Study of Religion and Islam: An Essay à propos of His *Opera Minora*," *Oriens* 21–22 (1968–69), 135–58; and Youakim Moubarac, *L'Oeuvre de Louis Massignon: Pentalogie Islamo-Chrétienne I* (Beirut: Editions du Cenacle Libanais, 1972–1973).

truly saintly scholar."[10] He was profoundly influenced by and promoted the ideas of Charles de Foucauld.

In October 1906 Massignon wrote to Foucauld (who had published *Reconnaissance au Maroc* to great acclaim in 1888–89), sending his thesis on Morocco. As a youth, Massignon had lost his faith (as had Foucauld). Foucauld promised to pray for him. Later, working near Baghdad, Massignon was kidnapped by fanatics and subsequently experienced "an ecstasy of fire and light, the certainty of the existence of God and Love."[11] (Foucauld's prayers answered?) The two met when Foucauld was in France in 1909. Brother Charles hoped Massignon would be "his spiritual heir . . . the longed-for companion who would assist him at Tamanrasset."[12] Family pressure and his spiritual director discouraged Massignon from going, though he and Brother Charles continued to correspond.

Foucauld returned to France in 1911 and again encouraged Massignon to join him in North Africa. The younger man was disposed to do so on a trial basis, but again, the family intervened. His father insisted he apply for a professorship at Lyon. Foucauld continued to await him, but in spite of encouragement from Paul Claudel, Massignon remained in France and eventually went to Cairo to lecture in the new Muslim university.[13] The two met once more in 1913. Massignon had decided to marry. Foucauld graciously wrote to him, "How great and beautiful, the mission of husband and wife!"[14]

While he never joined Foucauld in Morocco, Massignon was deeply influenced by Foucauld's spirituality and attitude toward Muslims. He wrote in 1917 of Foucauld's "contact with this dominant faith, which burns the believer to ashes beneath the

10. Griffith, "Merton, Massignon, and the Challenge of Islam," 57.

11. Quoted in Antier, *Charles de Foucauld*, 270. I rely on his biography of Foucauld for information on his relationship with Massignon.

12. Antier, *Charles de Foucauld*, 270–71.

13. For a more complete account see Antier, *Charles de Foucauld*, 269–96.

14. Quoted in Antier, *Charles de Foucauld*, 295.

unreachable sun of divine unity" which "acted as a catalyst to bring his unbelief back to Christian doctrine. . . ."[15] Spiritual relations between Christians and Muslims was Massignon's life's work, highlighting their shared beliefs and practices.[16] In 1924–28 "he played a major role in promoting interest in the ideals of Charles de Foucauld, including the publication of the latter's rule for religious life, *The Directory*."[17] Massignon's scholarship on Islam was enormously influential, the tap root of his opposition to France's Algerian war. He died in 1962, but not before corresponding with Thomas Merton, who was already familiar with Foucauld.

Massignon and Thomas Merton

Herbert Mason, an American doing research in Paris, introduced Merton and Massignon. In May 1959, Mason wrote Merton about his book *The Ascent to Truth* (1951) on St. John of the Cross. In August 1959, Mason wrote Merton about Massignon, enclosing his work on the legendary Seven Sleepers of Ephesus. Merton sent his article on Boris Pasternak, which Mason apparently shared with Massignon. By September 1959, Massignon was writing to Merton. The Thomas Merton Center at Bellarmine University (Louisville, Kentucky) has fourteen letters in English from Massignon between September 3, 1959, and April 26, 1961. Some of Merton's letters to Massignon appear in *Witness to Freedom: Letters in Times of Crisis*.[18]

Two factors facilitated the epistolary friendship. First, Thomas Merton was born in France and lived there as a child. (See part I, chap. 2, "Our Lady of the Museums," in his autobiography, *The Seven Storey Mountain* [1948].) He describes France as "the

---

15. Quoted in Antier, *Charles de Foucauld*, 93 and 118.

16. An example was his interest in the Seven Sleepers of Ephesus, mentioned in Sura 18 of the Holy Qur'an.

17. Griffith, "Merton, Massignon, and the Challenge of Islam," 55.

18. Thomas Merton, *Witness to Freedom: Letters in Times of Crisis* (ed. William H. Shannon; New York: Farrar, Straus, Giroux, 1994), 275–81.

fountains of the intellectual and spiritual life of the world to which I belonged."[19] Born and educated in France (and British secondary schools) and fluent in French, Merton was arguably a European, and knew Massignon's country and culture.

Second, Merton admired Charles de Foucauld.[20] Between 1947 and 1964 I counted some twenty references to Foucauld in Merton's letters and journals. Merton's March 9, 1950, journal entry indicates he is reading the spiritual notes of Foucauld, who "speaks to God in a clear and vibrant voice, simple words, sentences on fire. This voice rings in the ear of your heart after you have put the book away."[21] A March 18, 1960, letter to Massignon mentions both al-Hallaj and his "leaflet on Charles de Foucauld." [22] Merton's August 20, 1960, journal entry notes, "The voice and message of Charles de Foucauld mean very much to me. I think it is the most hopeful and living kind of message in our time."[23] On May 20, 1964, he wrote to James Forest (an American activist, writer, and a founder of the Catholic Peace Fellowship), "I am reading some fantastic stuff on Islam by Louis Massignon."[24]

Merton's *The Inner Experience: Notes on Contemplation*, a book with a complex history but first drafted in 1959, closes with an extended reflection on the Little Brothers of Jesus, founded by Voillaume, who was inspired by Foucauld. Merton

---

19. Thomas Merton, *The Seven Storey Mountain* (Garden City, NY: Doubleday/Image Books, 1970), 43.

20. See Bonnie Thurston, "'the most hopeful and living kind of message . . .': An Introduction to Charles de Foucauld and Thomas Merton," *The Merton Seasonal* 42, no. 2 (Summer 2017), 3–10.

21. Thomas Merton, *Entering the Silence,* Journals, Vol. 2, 1941–1952 (ed. Jonathan Montaldo; San Francisco: HarperSanFrancisco, 1996), 417.

22. Merton, *Witness to Freedom,* 276.

23. Thomas Merton, *Turning Toward the World*, Journals, Vol. 4 (1960–63) (ed. Victor A. Kramer; San Francisco: HarperSanFrancisco, 1997), 33.

24. Thomas Merton, *The Hidden Ground of Love: Letters* (ed. William H. Shannon; New York: Farrar, Straus, Giroux, 1985), 280.

concurs with their experiment in living contemplatively "like the laypeople around them . . . dedicated to God" and seeking "to imitate the hidden life of Jesus Christ at Nazareth,"[25] a clear reference to Foucauld. Of them Merton says, "where they are present, Christ is present."[26] These pages on Foucauld echo Merton's understanding of contemplation as he was exploring alternative monastic possibilities. What he hoped for himself echoed Foucauld's aspirations: to be a hermit/monk living a hidden life as a universal brother.

Professor Griffith summarizes the Massignon/Merton correspondence: both men were "searching for holiness," which includes addressing "the evils of their own societies."[27] Merton supported Massignon's work on behalf of North Africans in Paris and his opposition to the Algerian war. Massignon introduced Merton to the "mystical substitution" (mentioned above), and, most importantly, the Islamic concept of *le point vierge* in al-Hallaj. The Islamic understanding of the primordial or virgin point within humans appears repeatedly in Merton's writing in the 1960s. Merton writes to Massignon on July 20, 1960, it "moves me most of all."[28]

Because he did not write a book on Islam, Merton's engagement with it is not widely known. He knew the tradition well, and wrote in an October 31, 1967, letter of reading the Holy Qur'an, Avicenna, Ibn-Arabi, Ibn-Abbad, and Rumi.[29] Merton read the best available works on Islam in English and French. Although the talks are disappointing,[30] he lectured on Sufism to

---

25. Thomas Merton, *The Inner Experience: Notes on Contemplation* (ed. William F. Shannon; London: SPCK, 2003), 142.

26. Merton, *Inner Experience,* 142.

27. Griffith, "Merton, Massignon and the Challenge of Islam," 59.

28. Merton, *Witness to Freedom,* 278.

29. Merton, *Witness to Freedom,* 335.

30. Abdul Aziz wrote to William Shannon on May 10, 1986, that he was "shocked and disappointed about Merton's burlesque/parody of Sufism," in Griffith's "As One Spiritual Man to Another," 121. See Bernadette Dieker, "Merton's Sufi Lectures to Cistercian Novices, 1966–68," in *Merton and*

the monks at Gethsemani, and was especially interested in *jihad* (a spiritual term describing the struggle to conform one's will to God's), and the practices of *dhikr* (repetition of the Name) and *khalwah* (solitary retreat). He corresponded widely with Muslims and Islamic scholars.[31] There are seven poems on Islamic subjects in Merton's *Collected Poems*[32] and many references in his essays, letters, and journals.

In his journal on November 17, 1964, Merton wrote of Foucauld and Massignon: "both converted to Christianity by the witness of Islam to the one living God."[33] Foucauld influenced Massignon. Massignon influenced Merton. William Shannon notes, "it is clear that Massignon had a deep influence on Merton, who looked upon him as a spiritual mentor."[34] Massignon's letters to Merton encouraged the monk's Islamic interests. With al-Hallaj's idea of *le pointe vierge,* Massignon's most important gift to Merton was introducing him to Abdul Aziz. In correspondence with Aziz one encounters the depth of Merton's understanding of Islam and reads of his own prayer practice.

Sufism 130–62. Recordings of some of the lectures are on "Thomas Merton on Sufism," available at www.NowYouKnowMedia.com (2012). I cannot recommend them.

31. Reza Arasteh, Martin Lings, Louis Massignon, Herbert Mason, Abdul Aziz, Aly Abdel Ghani.

32. For more, see Patrick F. O'Connell, "Crescent Moon on the Eastern Horizon: Thomas Merton's Shorter Poems on Islamic themes," *The American Benedictine Review* 66, no. 3 (September 2015): 230–67; Erlinda Paguio, "Islamic Themes in Merton's Poetry," in *Merton and Sufism,* 89–100, and Bonnie Thurston, "Some Reflections on Merton's Islamic Poems" in Angus Stuart, ed., *Thomas Merton: The World in My Bloodstream* (Abergavenny, Wales: Three Peaks Press, 2004), 39–53.

33. Thomas Merton, *Dancing in the Water of Life,* Journals, Vol. 5, 1963–1965 (ed. Robert E. Daggy; San Francisco: HarperSanFrancisco, 1997), 166.

34. William H. Shannon, "Massignon, Louis," in *The Merton Encyclopedia* (ed. William H. Shannon, Christine M. Bochen, Patrick F. O'Connell; Maryknoll, NY: Orbis Books, 2002), 287.

MERTON AND ABDUL AZIZ[35]

In December 1951, Muslim Abdul Aziz asked a Roman Catholic colleague in Karachi to recommend a book on Christian mysticism. He suggested Thomas Merton's *The Ascent to Truth* (1951), which attempted to explain the mystical theology of St. John of the Cross in light of St. Thomas Aquinas. By Merton's own admission it was not a great success, but it led Herbert Mason to write to Merton, which led to the Merton–Massignon correspondence. Aziz received the book in February 1952, and soon thereafter began corresponding with Massignon. When Aziz mentioned Merton's book, Massignon suggested writing to Merton, who was also interested in al-Hallaj, which Aziz did on November 1, 1960. Merton responded on November 17, 1960. The correspondence continued until Merton's death in 1968. Seventeen of Merton's letters are preserved at Bellarmine University; fifteen appear (edited) in *The Hidden Ground of Love*.[36] The sixteen letters of Aziz at Bellarmine remain unpublished. Professor Griffith believes the "letters are unique"[37] in Islamic–Christian dialogue.

As with Massignon, biographical factors facilitated the friendship. Aziz was highly educated in the British system and lived through the turbulent years of the British withdrawal from India and the violent division of India and Pakistan. A devout Muslim, Aziz was a practicing Sufi. The two men were almost exact contemporaries, formed by British education and institutions. Both were devout practitioners of their own religious traditions.

---

35. The definitive essay is Griffith's "'As One Spiritual Man to Another,'" 101–29. See also Bonnie Bowman Thurston, "Brothers in Prayer and Worship: The Merton/Aziz Correspondence, An Islamic-Christian Dialogue," 17–33, in *The Voice of the Stranger,* essays delivered at the seventh general meeting of the Thomas Merton Society of Great Britain and Ireland, April 6–8, 2008, www.thomasmertonsociety.org.

36. Merton, *The Hidden Ground of Love*, 43–67.

37. Sidney H. Griffith, "Mystics and Sufi Masters: Thomas Merton and the Dialogue between Christians and Muslims," *Islam and Christian-Muslim Relations* 15, no. 3 (July 2004): 303.

Their deepest meeting points were Islamic and Christian prayer and mysticism in which both were well read and experientially knowledgeable. Each had read spiritual classics of the other's tradition and served as a reference service for the other, exchanging articles and books.

Aziz's letters initially exhibit the formality of English diplomacy. Merton writes less formal, less systematic responses. As the friendship develops, Aziz exhibits touching concern for Merton's health (giving advice about diet and rest). Merton wrote to other Muslims and Islamic scholars, but the Aziz letters are unique in their personal self-revelation. Affectionate openings and prayerful closings of the letters, often reflecting Islamic concepts, indicate how deeply the two understood *Tawhid* ("making one"). Merton's letters to Aziz reflect wide knowledge and deep understanding of Islam. The letter of January 2, 1966, details his daily life in his hermitage and his own method of meditation. To my knowledge it is the only autobiographical record we have of Merton's personal prayer practice.[38]

More could be said about the Aziz–Merton exchange. Lest we lose the thread of this essay, I introduce two reminders. First, clearly Merton's Christianity was enhanced by his engagement with Islam, just as Foucauld's and Massignon's had been, theirs by direct contact, Merton's secondarily through his association with them and directly through his friendship with Abdul Aziz. What Christine Bochen wrote of Merton is true of all four men: They had a "vocation to unity."[39] Although learned, their encounters were personal, spiritual, and transformative.

Second, the "hereditary line" from Foucauld to Merton is direct. Foucauld influenced Massignon who influenced Merton. Foucauld's profound encounter with and debt to Islam was

---

38. For more, see Bonnie Thurston, "'Rising Up Out of the Center': Thomas Merton on Prayer," *The Merton Annual* 20 (2007): 109–22, and chap. 7 in *Shaped by the End You Live For: Thomas Merton's Monastic Spirituality* (Collegeville, MN: Liturgical Press, 2020).

39. Christine Bochen, ed., *Thomas Merton: Essential Writings* (Maryknoll, NY: Orbis Press, 2000), 48.

mirrored in Massignon's experience. Both influenced Merton, Foucauld through Merton's reading and Massignon in their correspondence, which provided Merton with ideas that facilitated his dialogue with Abdul Aziz.

CONCLUSION

Outside human, linear time, God's work cannot be evaluated by its constraints. Merton wrote to James Forest, "Do not depend on the hope of results. When you are doing the sort of work you have taken on, essentially . . . apostolic work, you may have to face the fact that your work will be *apparently* worthless and even achieve no result at all"[40] (italics mine). In 1916, Foucauld's life's work *appeared* fruitless. But history demonstrates the church grows from the blood of her martyrs. Watered by his blood, the seed Foucauld planted in desert sand produced extraordinary fruit and ongoing possibilities for his essential work: bringing Christ to North Africa by living like him among his Muslim neighbors.

As St. Paul knew, and every gardener and farmer learns, gardening takes time and patience. One plants; another waters, "but only God . . . gives the growth" (1 Corinthians 3:6–7)—in God's "time." It takes time for the grape vine to mature, even longer for the wine produced from it. The influence of Foucauld on Massignon, who encouraged Merton, who engaged in dialogue with Abdul Aziz and developed an important set of principles for inter-religious dialogue,[41] extends over more than a century and continues.

What Merton wrote to Abdul Aziz in 1962 was true in Foucauld's day and is in ours: Muslim-Christian understanding "is something of very vital importance . . . and unfortunately it is rare and uncertain, or else subjected to the vagaries of

---

40. Merton, *Hidden Ground of Love*, 294.
41. See Appendix 4 and 5 in *The Asian Journal of Thomas Merton* (ed. N. Burton, P. Hart, and J. Laughlin; New York: New Directions, 1968/1975).

politics."[42] But those who confess the One God (*Tawhid*) can, for love of God, continue to water Foucauld's "vine," be nourished by his example, and, as he wrote, break "down . . . prejudices . . . through daily friendly relations, and changing . . . ideas by the manner and example of our lives."[43] Following Foucauld's example, living the "hidden life of Jesus," "the obscurity of a life hidden in God" and "where it will be of most service to [our] neighbor," we best care for his vine.[44] Foucauld recorded this word of Jesus during his retreat at Nazareth in November, 1897: "It is part of your vocation to proclaim the Gospel from the rooftops, not by what you say, but by how you live."[45] It was ever thus.

---

42. Merton, *The Hidden Ground of Love,* 53.

43. Jean-François Six, ed., *The Spiritual Autobiography of Charles de Foucauld* (trans. J. Holland Smith; Ijamsville, MD: Word Among Us Press, 2003), 181.

44. Foucauld, quoted in Six, *Spiritual Autobiography,* 83 and 167.

45. Robert Ellsberg, ed., *Charles de Foucauld* (Modern Spiritual Masters Series; Maryknoll, NY: Orbis Books, 1999), 79.

7

Charles de Foucauld, Louis Massignon, Catholic Spirituality, and Islam

Christian S. Krokus

At the conclusion of his book on the friendship between Charles de Foucauld (1858–1916) and Louis Massignon (1883–1962), Jean-François Six asks: "According to a reading of his letters to Massignon, what are the essential axes of Foucauldian spirituality? First of all, God is happy. He is never presented by Foucauld as a somber and terrible being, but as a being who possesses the fullness of joy."[1] Throughout his letters Foucauld most fre-

---

1. Jean-François Six, *L'Aventure de l'amour de dieu: 80 lettres inédites de Charles de Foucauld à Louis Massignon* (Paris: Éditions du Seuil, 1993), 236. Unless otherwise indicated, translations from French are my own. As I was putting the final touches on this article, it was revealed that after a two-year investigation a Vatican tribunal has convicted and defrocked Jean-François Six for having spiritually and sexually abused at least fifteen women from the 1950s through the 1990s. His name appears throughout the body and the footnotes of this article. Louis Massignon personally chose Jean-François Six to succeed him as director of the Union, and together with Mary Kahil he personally chose Six to succeed him as convener of the Paris Badaliya. It is horrible to have to mention such things, but in this era when the church is finally confronting its legacy of abuse and concealment, we cannot remain silent. There is also an opportunity, if we are open to it, for learning how to appropriate important Catholic figures critically, condemning, for example, the wicked behaviors of Six and the structures and theology that enabled them while appreciating the

63

quently refers to God as the Divine Lover, the Divine Spouse, or simply the Beloved. In one letter he writes: "Religion is all love. 'The Good Will of God toward men.' The first obligation is to love God; the second is to love one's neighbor as oneself for God."[2] Indeed it is remarkable how often Foucauld returns in those letters to the simplicity of love of God and love of neighbor, often adding the seemingly redundant specification: "How to acquire the love of God? By practicing charity toward men."[3] Foucauld thought of himself as Massignon's "older brother," and while the themes just mentioned are undoubtedly characteristic of Foucauld's spirituality in general, they also happen to be what his younger brother needed to hear.[4]

Both Foucauld and Massignon were converts to their native Catholic faith, but their conversion experiences were dramatically different. As Six observes, "The conversion of Charles de Foucauld occurred in an extremely simple way, one morning at the end of October 1886, through a peaceful confession at the gentle invitation of an admirable priest, followed by communion, all in an ordinary church. The conversion of Louis Massignon in 1908 is of a different kind."[5] There was nothing ordinary, peaceful, or gentle about Massignon's conversion experience. As a young man Massignon was involved in several homosexual encounters, including an ongoing relationship with the Spanish convert to Islam Luis de Cuadra (d. 1921). And whereas he once prided himself on transgressing social convention, in the turbulent days leading up to and through his May 1908 conversion he

---

scholarly, organizational, and even spiritual gifts he bequeathed to ours and subsequent generations. https://www.la-croix.com/Religion/Abus-sexuels-Jean-Francois-Six-renvoye-letat-clerical-2021-02-01-1201138298

2. January 31, 1912, in Six, *L'Aventure*, 120.

3. August 31, 1910, in Six, *L'Aventure*, 83. Foucauld was influenced by St. Francis de Sales (1567–1622) through the spiritual writer Abbé Antoine Crozier (1850–1916). See, for example, Six, *L'Aventure*, 93.

4. April 7, 1912 (Easter Sunday), in Six, *L'Aventure*, 126.

5. Six, *L'Aventure*, 39.

developed a keen sense of "good and evil."[6] Despairing of having committed acts of evil, he attempted to take his own life, and it was then that he experienced his well-known "Visitation of the Stranger," a conversion characterized in large part by a sense of being judged, deserving damnation, and being rescued from that fate only by the intercession of living and deceased witnesses, among them Charles de Foucauld, as Massignon understood it.[7]

In the aftermath of his conversion Massignon continued to be plagued by guilt and a near-compulsive urge to confess and to perform acts of penance, partly because he remained haunted by "temptations," presumably toward other men.[8] Such "temptations" feature prominently in the correspondence between Massignon and Foucauld, and here is where Foucauld applies his own understanding of God as a healing balm to Massignon's tortured soul. Time and again Foucauld writes a version of the following excerpt from his letter of July 15, 1916: "Let us review often the double history of the graces that God has granted to us personally since our birth and of our infidelities."[9] In other words, yes, acknowledge the missteps for which you are responsible, but do so always and only in the light of God's tender and understanding care, uninterruptedly present throughout your life. Foucauld often instructs Massignon, as in his letter of October 30, 1909: "Do not be surprised by temptations, dryness, or miseries," for "He puts our poor hearts through this ordeal in order to give us the opportunity to prove our love to him, to

---

6. Christian Destremau and Jean Moncelon, *Louis Massignon: le "cheikh admirable"* (Lectoure, France: Éditions Le Capucin, 2005), 85–86.

7. Louis Massignon, "Visitation of the Stranger: Response to an Inquiry about God," in *Testimonies and Reflections: Essays of Louis Massignon* (trans. Herbert Mason; Notre Dame, IN: University of Notre Dame Press, 1989), 39–42.

8. I do not, however, know with certainty exactly what Massignon and Foucauld discussed under the category of "temptations," a category along with many others in their correspondence that are likely drawn from the *Spiritual Exercises* of St. Ignatius of Loyola (1491–1556).

9. In Six, *L'Aventure*, 205.

strengthen it, to grow in virtue, and to become more worthy of him."[10]

Without denying their presence or severity, Foucauld never enters into the details of the temptations Massignon experienced. Instead he turns Massignon's attention away from himself and toward his neighbor: "Let us seek to redeem our sins a bit through love of neighbor. Doing good for others is an excellent remedy to temptations. It is to pass from defense to counterattack."[11] There will be falls, but it is important to remember that "if one succumbs to a temptation, it is not that one does not love at all but that one's love is too weak, in which case one must cry like St. Peter and be humbled like him. However, also like him, one must say three times: 'I love you. I love you. You know that despite my weaknesses and sins, I love you.'"[12]

Nowhere is Foucauld's compassionate counsel more evident than in his response to Massignon's decision to marry rather than to join him at Tamanrasset. Massignon was Foucauld's best hope for finding a companion and a successor. The news must have been terribly disappointing to him, but there is not a hint of it in his subsequent letters.[13] Knowing Massignon's struggles with sexuality as well as his penchant for dwelling on past sins, and perhaps knowing Massignon's confessed "misogyny,"[14] Foucauld counseled his younger confrère: "If God wants marriage for you, do not accept it as an expiation but as the state in which he has reserved the most graces for you. . . . [W]hat a grand and admirable vocation! And how good to be a married saint in the world, penetrating into spaces where the priest hardly enters and penetrating with an intimacy rarely possible

10. In Six, *L'Aventure*, 67.

11. July 15, 1916, in Six, *L'Aventure*, 206.

12. July 15, 1916, in Six, *L'Aventure*, 205.

13. The contrast with the disparaging, dismissive, and sarcastic response of Paul Claudel to the same news is particularly striking. See Six, *L'Aventure*, 151, 162, 183.

14. Destremau, *Louis Massignon*, 124.

for a priest."[15] A major thread in Foucauld's letters therefore is that of an experienced Christian counseling a recent convert toward trust in a loving God, gentleness with himself, and compassionate kindness toward others.

There is, however, another thread that became prominent in the later letters where Foucauld sometimes glorifies danger, violence, and even death. When World War I began, Massignon, recently married and with a child on the way, hesitated to join the effort but was persuaded by friends to take a position in Paris with the Ministry of Foreign Affairs.[16] When he requested active duty at the Dardanelles Foucauld commended him for his courage: "I approve absolutely. Remain at the front until the end." He continued: "With respect to the sacrifices to be made and the duties to be fulfilled, we should always be in the front row."[17] In what he called "a feeble attempt to show him that I had not deserted his call," Massignon informed Foucauld of his next request for an even more dangerous assignment in the trenches on the Serbian front.[18] Once again Foucauld approved. In his letter of December 1, 1916, just hours before he was killed, Foucauld wrote: "You did very well to ask to join the troop. We should never hesitate to request the posts where the danger, the sacrifice, and the dedication are the greatest. Let us leave the honor to whoever wants it, but the danger and the pain, let us

---

15. September 30, 1913, in Six, *L'Aventure*, 154. Christian Destremau speculates that Massignon was influenced by Anne-Catherine Emmerich, who said, "Marriage is a state of penance" (Destremau, *Louis Massignon*, 133).

16. See Destremau, *Louis Massignon*, 139–40.

17. June 1, 1916, in Six, *L'Aventure*, 204. See also the letters of June 29, 1915 (187), July 15, 1915 (188), and September 8, 1915 (189).

18. Louis Massignon, "An Entire Life with a Brother Who Set Out on the Desert: Charles de Foucauld," in Massignon, *Testimonies*, 28. On Massignon's "expiation" for not joining Foucauld at Tamanrasset, see also Paolo Dall'Oglio, "Massignon and *ǧihād* in the Light of de Foucauld, al-Ḥallāǧ and Gandhi," in *Faith, Power, and Violence: Muslims and Christians in a Plural Society, Past and Present* (ed. John Donohue and Christian Troll; Rome: Pontificio Istituto Orientale, 1998), 103–14.

always claim them. Christians must provide the example of sacrifice and dedication. It is a principle to which we must be faithful for all our lives, simply, without asking ourselves whether there is pride in our conduct. It is our duty."[19] After advising Massignon not to worry about his family, promising that God would protect his wife and child should he be killed in action, he insists: "Walk this way in simplicity and peace, certain that it is JESUS who inspired you to follow it."[20]

The mix of violence and religious sentiment is thoroughgoing in those late letters. Foucauld described the war as a "crusade" and a "religious duty."[21] He argued that the wickedness of the Germans "put them beyond the law."[22] He encouraged Massignon to think of himself as participating in Jesus's saving mission, "even by arms and combat, for the present war is a crusade against the paganism and barbarity of the Germans. You save future generations by defending them against the invasion of these anti-Christian doctrines."[23] His disparagement of the Germans was matched only by his confidence in the virtue, rightness, and even holiness of the French: "We should be happy at being born French and for being on the side of law and justice, on the side that fights in order that Christian morality remains and becomes ever more the law of the world."[24]

Even outside the direct context of war, as Massignon observed, Foucauld sometimes said things "not very compatible with his priesthood." For example, after a local raid resulted in the death of a young officer whom Foucauld respected, he demanded vengeance, hoping soldiers would catch the organizer and "put twelve bullets in his skin."[25] He also long experienced a desire

19. In Six, *L'Aventure*, 214.
20. In Six, *L'Aventure*, 214.
21. December 6, 1915, in Six, *L'Aventure*, 195.
22. January 12, 1916, in Six, *L'Aventure*, 197.
23. September 15, 1916, in Six, *L'Aventure*, 212.
24. March 6, 1916, in Six, *L'Aventure*, 200.
25. Louis Massignon, "Foucauld au desert devant le dieu d'Abraham, Agar, et Ismaël," in *Écrits mémorables* [hereinafter *EM*], vol. 1 (ed.

for martyrdom. In an oft-quoted passage from a meditation of 1897, Foucauld writes in the voice of Jesus: "Remember that you ought to die as a martyr, stripped of everything, stretched naked on the ground, unrecognizable, covered with wounds and blood, killed violently and painfully—and desire that it be today."[26] If his description of a whole nation as "beyond the law" and as deserving of destruction contradicts his emphasis on a loving, gentle, forgiving God, then his desire for martyrdom, embrace of the cross, and encouragement of sacrifice, while not rising to the same level of contradiction, at least sit in tension with his devotion to the God who rejoices in love and family and the ordinary currents of life, the God who rejoices in Nazareth.

In various talks and publications Massignon passed along much of the tender spiritual wisdom he received in Foucauld's letters. For example, in the Badaliya convocation of January 5, 1962, he advised: "Remember, Foucauld wrote to us to go frequently over the double history (within yourselves) of the graces received from God and of our infidelities."[27] In an article that would become an appendix to the 1961 edition of the *Directory*,[28] Massignon quoted another line that appears regularly in Foucauld's letters: "One achieves good, not to the extent of what one says or does, but to the extent of who one is—to the extent

---

Christian Jambet, François Angelier, François L'Yvonnet, and Souâd Ayada; Paris: Éditions Robert Laffont, 2009), 112.

26. Charles de Foucauld, *Charles de Foucauld: Writings* (ed. Robert Ellsberg; Maryknoll, NY: Orbis Books, 1999), 77. See also, for instance, Charles de Foucauld, *Scriptural Meditations on Faith* (trans. Alexandra Russell; New York: New City Press, 1988), 129–30; Charles de Foucauld, *Meditations of a Hermit* (trans. Charlotte Balfour; Maryknoll, NY: Orbis Books, 1981), 186.

27. Louis Massignon, *Louis Massignon: A Pioneer of Interfaith Dialogue/The Badaliya Prayer Movement* (ed. Dorothy Buck; Clifton, NJ: Blue Dome Press, 2016), 264.

28. For a summary of Massignon's role in the spiritual legacy of Foucauld, see Jacques Keryell, "Louis Massignon et l'Association Charles de Foucauld," in *Louis Massignon au coeur de notre temps* (ed. Jacques Keryell; Paris: Éditions Karthala, 1999), 173–93.

that grace accompanies our acts, to the extent that our acts are
the acts of Jesus acting in us and through us."[29] Most importantly, inspired by Foucauld, Massignon called the Badaliya to
live as the "poor amongst the most poor."[30] He develops that last
point at some length in a 1959 Sorbonne tribute to Foucauld.
He writes: "I feel obligated to explain to you how, through this
living experience of the sacred in others, Foucauld was given
to me like an older brother and how he helped me to find my
brothers in all other human beings, starting with the most abandoned ones." He continues: "I needed him to communicate to
me, through spiritual contact, in very simple words, by inter-
views and letters, his experiential initiation into the real understanding of the human condition, his experiential knowledge of
the compassion which drew him and committed him to the most
abandoned of human beings."[31] The influence was not merely
pastoral. Ariana Patey has shown how this lesson in experiential compassion translated into Massignon's scholarly study of
mysticism.[32]

Predominantly, however, Massignon emphasized Foucauld's
attraction to danger and his desire for martyrdom, as well as
the circumstances surrounding his actual death. He learned from
Foucauld that to follow Jesus means "imitating Him as much in
His death as in his life."[33] He read Foucauld's passages on the
love of God through the lens of the cross: "Love is defined by its
formal object, and, when it has God for its object, it necessarily

---

29. Louis Massignon, "L'Union de prières pour le développement de
l'esprit missionnaire surtout en faveur des colonies françaises," *EM* 1: 102.

30. Convocation #56—June 5, 1959, in Massignon, *Badaliya Prayer
Movement*, 174.

31. Massignon, "Entire Life," 22.

32. Ariana Patey, "The Life and Thought of Charles de Foucauld:
A Christian Eremitical Vocation to Islam and His Contribution to the
Understanding of Muslim-Christian Relations within the Catholic
Tradition" (Ph.D. thesis, Heythrop College, University of London, 2012),
251.

33. Massignon, "L'Union de prières," 103–4.

receives the form of Christ's passion, and it is configured as such from the Last Supper to the Cross."[34] He seemed also to turn Foucauld's particular advice regarding moments of temptation into a general principle: "Make with Jesus to his Father a declaration of love, of pure love, in the spiritual dryness, the night, the estrangement, the appearance of abandonment, the self-doubt, in all the bitterness of love, without any of its sweetness."[35] Just as one cannot separate Nazareth from the cross in the life of Jesus, neither in the life of Charles de Foucauld can one separate Nazareth from his own martyrdom. It was the former that prepared him for the latter: "The hidden life in the house of Nazareth, this humble and modest grace, within reach of everyone, slowly, gently, and surely led Foucauld to the final heroism."[36] Finally, it is primarily Foucauld's martyrdom that makes him an inspirational source for the orientation of the Badaliya as articulated in the 1947 statutes:

> [I]t is up to us to continue the attitude of Saint Francis and Saint Louis towards those millions of souls who wait for us and look towards us; to we who are called to give testimony with our lives, and if God permits with our death, like Foucauld, who obtained martyrdom and even asked for it for his friends: to give to this Christ, who asks us to continue his passion, that *shahada* that we desire to offer to him, as unworthy of it as we are.[37]

In Massignon's appropriation of Foucauld's spirituality the inherent tension is almost completely resolved in favor of the cross.

The entire collection of eighty letters he received from Foucauld has been described as being for Massignon an "almost sacramental sign of his vocation as executor," but it is the last

---

34. Louis Massignon, "Plus qu'un anneau scelle au doigt," *EM* 1: 120.
35. Massignon, "Entire Life," 29.
36. Massignon, "L'Union de prières," 102.
37. Massignon, *Badaliya Prayer Movement*, 3.

letter that held pride of place.[38] Foucauld wrote that letter just hours before he was murdered. In it he prays for the safety of Massignon, who was at that time fighting in the trenches, and he reports of his own situation: "Our corner of the Sahara is at peace." Massignon describes the moment he learned of Foucauld's death: "Beside myself, I climbed onto the parapet of the snow-covered trench, seized by a feeling of sacred joy, and cried out: 'He found his way, he succeeded!'"[39] The incongruity of their respective fates was not lost on Massignon: "By a strange switch, he was killed and I was protected."[40] Once again, as he had at his conversion, Foucauld saved him, but that only redoubled Massignon's sense of obligation to seek danger, for himself and with the members of the Badaliya:

> The work of mercy to which we have been invited is to try to respond to [the Muslims'] clamor for justice (*sayha bi'l-haqq*) by entering into their most painful matters of conscience, when they entrust us with them in friendship. It is that "go to the Front" that Foucauld called us to in his last letter: "One must never hesitate to ask for the posts where the danger, the sacrifice and the devotion are the most. Leave honor to those who desire it, but always ask for danger and pain." There is the true Arab "jihad akbar," this "holy War" leading to suffering from the same faults in the depth of himself that we want to make up for, to atone. Such substitution, "Badaliya," goes very far.[41]

That Foucauld's own dangerous adventure in the Sahara ended in so inglorious a fashion, alone and without "any grand

---

38. Hugues Didier, "Louis Massignon and Charles de Foucauld," *ARAM* 20 (2008): 345.

39. Massignon, "Entire Life," 28.

40. Massignon, "Entire Life," 28.

41. Annual Letter 1, in Massignon, *Badaliya Prayer Movement*, 9. For the oft-told story of Massignon being attacked while delivering a lecture on Foucauld, see Six, *L'Aventure*, 302–3.

material results," as Massignon put it, was, as they say, not a bug but a feature.[42] First of all, it identified him with the abandoned Jesus: "Foucauld led me to understand, in his lifetime, but above all by his death, that the priest is a deposit of the alms of eternal hospitality, which was bequeathed to him by one condemned to death at the moment he was betrayed, delivered, and executed."[43] Many of the religious figures to whom Massignon was attracted were martyrs and stigmatics; many of them were women who experienced horrible ailments or extreme physical penances, and none of them was considered a grand success at the end of her or his life.[44] They include Blessed Anne Catherine Emmerich (1774–1824), Violet Susman (d. 1950), Marie des Vallées (1590–1656), St. Christine the Admirable (1150–1224), and St. Joan of Arc (1412–1431), as well as Joris-Karl Huysmans (1848–1907), St. Francis of Assisi (1182–1226), the Seven Sleepers of Ephesus (fourth century), and, outside the Christian tradition, Gandhi (1869–1948) and Hallaj (858–922), just to name a few. Most Catholics and Muslims would consider those figures to be obscure, if not dangerous in their embrace of suffering, but to Massignon they were the "real elite," the hidden spiritual pillars of history and society, the substitute saints, and Foucauld belonged among them.[45] He joins those who, like Abraham before Sodom, intercede with God on behalf of their respective sinful communities, and who with Jesus offer themselves to God as willing and nonviolent sacrifices on behalf of others. Hence Massignon could compare Foucauld to "Job the Patient . . . who became docile, in the most noble way, not as an abject slave under the whip of his master, but thanks to an interior comprehension, infused with fertile sadness, of a conception

---

42. Massignon, "Entire Life," 29.

43. Massignon, "Foucauld au desert," 114.

44. St. Francis of Assisi may seem to be an exception, but in Louis Massignon's vision Francis's reception of the stigmata at Alvernia was the result of his failure to convert the sultan at Damietta.

45. See Louis Massignon, "The Notion of 'Real Elite' in Sociology and in History," in Massignon, *Testimonies*, 57–64.

of human solidarity, even more, of a filial ransom to the Justice of God."[46] Foucauld was a "hostage and ransom, the guarantee of our Christian loyalty to the Muslims for whom the Guest is sacred."[47]

Massignon's inclusion of Foucauld among the substitute saints is complicated by two inconvenient facts. First, although he was technically unarmed at the moment of his death, it is a stretch to say that he was a nonviolent and willing victim. Foucauld had fortified his hermitage with rifles and ammunition, preparing with the men of the village to fend off attacks by German- or Ottoman-trained militias. Plus, he volunteered to be mobilized and likely helped to coordinate the French Saharan defense. In the end he was lured out of his fort by a familiar voice, and was shot and killed, probably unintentionally, by a panicked fifteen-year-old boy. However, as Hugues Didier has remarked, "Foucauld could well have died with a weapon in his hands instead of being assassinated. And he would have done it *out of duty*."[48]

Working with the fact that Foucauld did not have a weapon in his hand, Massignon developed a creative interpretation of the scene: "[I]f he decided at the end to keep a weapon in his Borj, he who had vowed never to have any weapon in his cell, it was because he was giving to his enemies 'full dispensation to shed his blood' in a lawful sacrifice." He continues: "Foucauld changed for them in advance the designation of their murderous act: 'Be the fighters of a holy war, and I will die a martyr.' He was thereby entering into their hearts as an inebriating wine."[49] In other words, it was not they who lured Foucauld out of the fort but Foucauld who lured them into taking his life; and in advance he knowingly and deliberately created the conditions that would allow his murderers to claim self-defense and thus to

46. Louis Massignon, "La douceur, qui naît des larmes, au desert," *EM* 1: 121.
47. Massignon, "Foucauld au desert," 114.
48. Didier, "Louis Massignon," 341.
49. Massignon, "Entire Life," 31.

remain innocent before the human and divine law: "God would not be able to damn them, since he, their victim, forgave them."[50]

The second inconvenience has to do with Islam. Foucauld undoubtedly loved his Touareg neighbors, but he was not enamored of Islam per se in the way that Massignon was.[51] Although he was attracted to Islam as a young man, and although Massignon regularly points to Foucauld's reverent treatment of the *Laylat al-Qadr* in his *Reconnaissance au Maroc* (1888),[52] it remains that under the advice of his spiritual director Foucauld deliberately "fled Islam just as it is appropriate to flee a temptation."[53] He typically referred to Muslims as infidels; it has been said that he "hated the shari'a," and his writings are filled with calls for the conversion of Muslims in French colonies, albeit by gentle, patient, loving means.[54] When Massignon shared with him an early sketch of his understanding of Muslims as spiritual siblings in Abraham, Foucauld responded: "I would suppress the first point: meditation on the vocation given to the sons of Abraham and his servant. This can never be proven, and since Our Lord, all people have the vocation to be Christians."[55] Massignon rightly felt disappointed and misunderstood, so how could Foucauld be a model for the Badaliya whose members offered their lives for Muslims, "not so they would be converted,

---

50. Massignon, "L'Union de prières," 93.

51. For a Muslim appreciation of the life of Charles de Foucauld, see Ali Merad, *Christian Hermit in an Islamic World: A Muslim's View of Charles de Foucauld* (ed. Zoe Hersov; Mahwah, NJ: Paulist Press, 2000). For some implications of that appreciation, see Zoe Hersov, "A Muslim's View of Charles de Foucauld: Some Lessons for the Christian-Muslim Dialogue," *Muslim World* 85, nos. 3–4 (July–October 1995): 295–316.

52. See, for example, Annual Letter 10, in Massignon, *Badaliya Prayer Movement*, 99.

53. Didier, "Louis Massignon," 350.

54. Didier, "Louis Massignon," 351. See also Minlib Dallh, "Exploration in Mysticism and Religious Encounter: The Case of Charles de Foucauld (1858–1916)," *The Downside Review* 138, no. 4 (2020): 139.

55. July 15, 1916, in Six, *L'Aventure*, 206.

but so that the will of God might be accomplished in them and through them"?[56]

Despite recognizing that Foucauld had not entered Islam "axially" as he had,[57] Massignon argued that it was "the whole mass of Muslim faithful for whom he died."[58] Massignon's claim once again employed a creative interpretation, this time of the symbolic context in which the death took place. Not only was Foucauld killed by Muslims, but near his dead body was found his monstrance with the exposed Host, which told Massignon that Foucauld's last hours were spent not only in writing letters but also in meditation on the self-offering of Christ.[59] His death was therefore linked to that of Jesus, who "gave himself completely broken and dying to make us live again, we his enemies, his murderers."[60] Plus, according to Massignon, even though Foucauld spent his life immersed in Berber, his last words were uttered in Arabic, the sacred language of Islam: "I am going (or I wish) to die."[61] Foucauld had therefore come to understand his end as a self-offering on behalf of *his* enemies and *his* murderers, namely, the Muslims. Massignon was not naïve about the interpretive leaps he was taking. He recognized that "Foucauld did not immediately understand his profound vocation as victim and intercessor and, I would say, as a saint 'Islamized by his death.'"[62] It was Foucauld, however, who taught him that "one does not choose a vocation; one receives it."[63] If Foucauld did not fully recognize his own vocation, "his work remains incomplete, and it is for us to perfect it."[64] For example, Fou-

---

56. Mary Louise Gude, *Louis Massignon: The Crucible of Compassion* (Notre Dame, IN: University of Notre Dame Press, 1996), 134–35.
57. Massignon, "Foucauld au desert," 107.
58. Massignon, "Entire Life," 30.
59. Massignon, "Plus qu'un anneau scelle au doigt," 119.
60. Massignon, "Entire Life," 31.
61. Massignon, "Entire Life," 26.
62. Massignon, "Foucauld au desert," 109.
63. Massignon, "Plus qu'un anneau scelle au doigt," 119.
64. Massignon, "Plus qu'un anneau scelle au doigt," 119.

cauld may have identified with the most abandoned, but it was Massignon who realized "that the most abandoned of people . . . are the Muslims: these mysterious people excluded from the divine preferences in history, though the sons of Abraham, and driven into the desert with Ishmael and Hagar."[65] He therefore felt responsible, as he wrote in a 1954 letter to Mary Kahil (1889–1979), to "complete him in the Badaliya where we love our Muslim brothers in his place, more than him."[66]

Jean-François Six has credited Charles de Foucauld, along with his contemporary St. Thérèse of Lisieux (1873–97), with being instrumental in effecting a shift in French, Catholic spirituality from a focus on God as Judge to one on God as Love.[67] There exists a tension, however, with his belief in a God who desires martyrdom and justifies violence, with his willingness to dismiss concerns about acting with pride, with his certainty about knowing Jesus's will in favor of violence, and with his confidence in French moral superiority; but it is nonetheless true that his letters to Louis Massignon reveal that Foucauld was mostly centered in God's attractive, gentle, healing, merciful, love. At the same time, Massignon considered himself to be Foucauld's spiritual "heir,"[68] and it is true that he was deeply influenced by Foucauld's eremitical immersion among the most abandoned,[69] his ability to see the sacred in every human being, his vision of Christians joined in a union of prayers, his recognition of God's work in the hidden life of Nazareth, his understanding of the Gospel as an invitation to join in Jesus's saving mission, and his willingness to "go to the front" if that is what God desires; but it cannot be said that Massignon, who once described prayer as

---

65. Massignon, "Entire Life," 22.

66. Louis Massignon, *L'Hospitalité sacrée* (ed. Jacques Keryell; Paris: Nouvelle Cité, 1987), 290.

67. Six, *L'Aventure*, 207.

68. Louis Massignon, "Les maîtres qui ont guidé ma vie," *Horizons Maghrebins* 14–15 (1989): 159.

69. See chapter 7 of Ariana Patey's aforementioned PhD dissertation, "The Life and Thought of Charles de Foucauld," 39–77.

the "daughter of the fear of both the Judgment and the Judge,"[70] appropriated his teacher's tender relationship with the gentle Divine Lover.[71] The contrast can be highlighted briefly with three images.

First, like some other prominent Parisian intellectuals of his day, Massignon was attracted to the reported apparition of La Salette, in part because of the associated themes of warning, judgment, and punishment in relation to lukewarm Catholic belief and practice. When he asked Foucauld's opinion on the matter, the latter replied: "You asked what I think of Sister Marie of the Cross (Mélanie de la Salette)—My dear brother, I do not think anything. If Rome makes a decision on the subject, then I will follow what Rome says. I regard it as a fault—the fault of using time badly or of losing time—to spend time on this when so many souls do not know JESUS and their salvation depends on knowing Him." He continues: "Dear brother, stick to the simple things. Remember always and practically the divine word: The first commandment is to love God with all one's heart, and the second is to love one's neighbor as oneself. Everything is there and we must constantly return there. My children, love one another. That is the Master's precept, and it is enough."[72]

Second, when in 1903 his friend Dr. Hérisson asked him how best to win the affection of the Touareg, Foucauld responded: "You must be simple, affable and kind. . . . In order to be loved, you must love them and make them feel that you love them. Don't be an adjutant or a doctor with them, and don't be offended by their familiarity or their easy manner. Be human, charitable, and always cheerful. You must always laugh, even

---

70. Louis Massignon, "The Three Prayers of Abraham," in Massignon, *Testimonies*, 4.

71. For a first-hand account of the deepening post-mortem influence of Foucauld upon Massignon, see René Voillaume, "In Memoriam Louis Massignon," in *Presence de Louis Massignon: Hommages et témoignages* (Paris: Éditions Maisonneuve et Larose, 1987), 179–83.

72. March 10, 1912, in Six, *L'Aventure*, 125.

in saying simple things. I, as you will see, laugh all the time, showing my bad teeth. Laughter creates good humor with them. It brings men closer together and helps them understand each other better. It cheers up a glum atmosphere, and that is a charity. When you are with Touaregs, always laugh."[73] Compare Foucauld's exhortation to laugh and to cheer up a glum situation with a heartbreaking excerpt from a 1960 letter that Louis Massignon wrote to Thomas Merton (1915–1968): "My case is not to be imitated; I made a duel with our Lord and having been an outlaw (against nature in love), against law (substituted to Muslims) and Hierarchy . . . (leaving my native proud Latin community for a despised, bribed and insignificant Greek Catholic Melkite church), I die lonely in my family, for whom I am a bore. . . . I am a gloomy scoundrel."[74]

Third, the tension in Foucauld's spirituality is neatly captured in the image he designed of a cross above a heart accompanied by the words "Jesus Caritas." It seems to represent both Foucauld's insistence that one review the divine graces and the personal infidelities of one's history as well as his twin attractions to the loving God and to martyrdom. As part of his mission to "complete" Foucauld, Massignon felt compelled to modify that image for the Badaliya: "He designed [the heart] asymmetrically, in order to show that it was living. And he adjoined the two words: 'Jesus Caritas.' [However] after having meditated, at Ephesus, in the country of the Dormition where the three witnesses of the thrust of the lance founded in solitude the Church of Contemplatives, it came to us that this blazon should be more precise. It was in 1953, praying for the Morocco that Foucauld so loved, that we understood that this heart must be 'stigmatized' and the script written in Arabic: 'Yasu' / ibn / Maryam / Huwa l-Hubbu,' 'Jesus / son of / Mary / He is love.'"[75] On the

73. Jean-François Six, *Witness in the Desert: The Life of Charles de Foucauld* (trans. Lucie Noel; New York: Macmillan, 1965), 178.

74. Quoted in Sidney Griffith, "Thomas Merton, Louis Massignon, and the Challenge of Islam," *The Merton Annual* 3 (1990): 172.

75. Louis Massignon, "La blessure au côté," *EM* 1: 123.

one hand, it is as though the cross is not enough to represent the pains of the world. Even the heart must be pierced. The substitutes know that, whether human or divine, love is always wounded and always involves suffering and sacrifice. On the other hand, Massignon's translation of Foucauld's motto is not simply into the language of Arabic but into the language of the Qur'an, where Jesus is known as the Son of Mary. It is a profound spiritual and theological gesture on behalf of a Catholic sodality, recognizing that Jesus is shared among Christians and Muslims and that the church has an obligation to find some way to engage with Muslims not as rivals but as siblings.[76] If Charles de Foucauld's canonization represents for the church an embrace of "universal brotherhood," and a willingness, humbly, to be dependent upon and even saved by and through our neighbors,[77] one must not lose sight of Louis Massignon's role in preserving and disseminating Foucauld's gifts as well as his own decisive role in the conversion of the church's approach to Muslims as taught in *Nostra Aetate*.[78]

---

76. For a treatment of the ways Massignon theologically went beyond Foucauld as well as key differences between the Union and the Badaliya, see Paolo Dall'Oglio, "Louis Massignon and Badaliya," *ARAM* 20 (2008): 329–36.

77. In 1908 Foucauld became terribly ill. He was in desperate need of nourishment, and even though the region was suffering under a severe drought, Foucauld's Touareg neighbors extracted whatever milk was available from the local goats and brought it to Foucauld. They nursed him back to health, and Foucauld apparently learned that he was even more dependent on his neighbors than they were on him. See Charles Lepetit, *Two Dancers in the Desert: The Life of Charles de Foucauld* (Maryknoll, NY: Orbis Books, 1983), 65.

78. See Christian Krokus, "Louis Massignon's Influence on the Teaching of Vatican II on Muslims and Islam," *Islam and Christian-Muslim Relations* 3 (2012): 329–45. See also Isabel Olizar, "From the Margins to the Center: Exploring *Nostra Aetate* in the Lives of Charles de Foucauld, Louis Massignon, and Pierre Claverie," in *Nostra Aetate, Non-Christian Religions, and Interfaith Relations* (ed. Kail Ellis; New York: Palgrave Macmillan, 2020), 138–61.

8

St. Francis of Assisi and St. Charles de Foucauld: Incarnation, a Relationship of Love with All Creation

Patrick Carolan

In writing his encyclical *Fratelli tutti: On Fraternity and Social Friendship*, Pope Francis mentions being motivated by the Grand Imam Ahmad Al-Tayyeb, whom, as he writes, "I met in Abu Dhabi, where we declared that 'God has created all human beings equal in rights, duties and dignity, and has called them to live together as brothers and sisters.'" The grand imam followed up by tweeting, "My brother, Pope Francis's message, *Fratelli tutti*, is an extension of the Document on Human Fraternity, and reveals a global reality in which the vulnerable and marginalized pay the price for unstable positions and decisions. . . It is a message that is directed to people of good will, whose consciences are alive and restores to humanity consciousness." Pope Francis and Al-Tayyeb co-signed the Document on Human Fraternity for World Peace and Living Together in February 2019 in Abu Dhabi. As he did in *Laudato Si'*, Pope Francis wrote this encyclical through the lens of Christianity but with a desire "to make this reflection an invitation to dialogue among all people of good will."

Pope Francis starts his encyclical reflecting on St. Francis of Assisi and concludes it with a dedication to Blessed (now St.)

Charles de Foucauld. It is fitting that, in writing an encyclical on friendship and the connectedness of all, Pope Francis should refer to and cite these two holy men. While their lives were separated by some seven hundred years their message, actions and stories are deeply connected. As Father Diego Fares SJ wrote in *Catholic Outreach*: "The figure of the soon-to-be-canonized Charles de Foucauld serves as a great testimonial force in *Fratelli tutti*: he gathers and updates the legacy of Francis of Assisi, synthesizes and embodies the Gospel content that the pope repeats in the encyclical, and challenges us concretely wherever the greatest issues of our time arise."

In many regards the life of Charles de Foucauld somewhat paralleled that of Francis of Assisi. Both men were born into families that were considered upper class or wealthy. Both made the choice to join the military and go off to war. Despite being raised Catholic, neither was very religious in his early life. Both had a transformative experience that led them on a spiritual journey. Both had encounters with Muslims. In all probability, both initially set out to convert Muslims to Christianity. Neither was successful at his attempts but instead developed a deeper understanding and appreciation of Islam and attributed to these encounters the strengthening of his own Christian faith. They are both considered to be among the pillars of interfaith relationships. The twentieth-century pioneer of interfaith relations Louis Massignon considered St. Francis and St. Charles to have had the greatest influence on his work.

St. Francis was born in the small town of Assisi in 1182. He was the son of a wealthy cloth merchant. He would have received a basic education but not attended advanced college. He also would have received formal religious education as part of the Church of St. Giorgio of Assisi. His father being wealthy would have probably had a close relationship with the bishop and been considered a leader around town. His mother came from a noble family. Francis grew up more interested in fine clothes, dancing, singing, and drinking wine than in church or business. He was expected to follow in his father's footsteps.

But he much preferred spending time frolicking with his friends. He dreamed of going off to war and becoming a great knight. When he was 20, war broke out between the city-state of Assisi and its neighbor Perugia. In his early years he was trained and skilled in archery and swordsmanship. He finally was going to have the chance to live his dream and become a famous valiant knight. Fortunately for us, as is often the case, things didn't work out the way Francis had planned. He was captured and held prisoner for a year until his father paid a ransom to free him. One can only imagine if things turned out differently. If Francis and Assisi had been successful and defeated Perugia, Francis would have returned not a broken, beaten young man but a glorious hero. Years later, instead of going to Damietta to try and bring about peace between Christians and Muslims, he in all likelihood would have been there as a knight fighting for the Christians against the Muslims. Though he was considered to be courteous, respectful, and kind to the poor, his early life gave no indication that he would become one of the most transformative figures in history.

The church at the time of Francis had gone through a dramatic change and evolution. Author and activist Brian McLaren describes it this way: "Christianity began as a revolutionary nonviolent movement promoting a new kind of aliveness on the margins of society. . . . It claimed that everyone, not just an elite few, had God-given gifts to use for the common good. It exposed a system based on domination, privilege, and violence and proclaimed in its place a vision of mutual service, mutual responsibility, and peaceable neighborliness. It put people above profit, and made the audacious claim that the Earth belonged not to rich tycoons or powerful politicians, but to the Creator who loves every sparrow in the trees and every wildflower in the field. It was a peace movement, a love movement, a joy movement, a justice movement, an integrity movement, an aliveness movement." But after Constantine and the Council of Nicaea Christianity began to change. It stopped being a movement for the poor and marginalized focused on building God's kingdom on Earth into a religion for the rich and powerful. As the church grew, it became intertwined with forming alliances with kings and princes and less interested in helping the poor. As popes grew in popularity and power, they also began to accumulate great wealth. In 800, Pope Leo III crowned Charlemagne, the ruler of the Carolingian Empire, as emperor of what would later be known as the Holy Roman Empire. This helped unite Western Europe and cemented the pope's position as a powerful political force to be reckoned with.

When Francis was born, the church was a powerful, wealthy organization that could make or break a leader depending on the whim of the pope. Its essence was a focus on laws and doctrine interpreted, delivered, and controlled by the pope and his bishops and priests. It was believed and taught that laws and doctrines were divinely given to the hierarchy and handed down through time from God. Therefore, they were not open to discussion or debate. In 1095, Pope Urban II declared a holy crusade to recapture Jerusalem and either convert or destroy the infidel Muslims. He called on nobles and knights to lead and everyone from soldiers to farmers to join and fight. Pope Urban declared an armed pilgrimage in which participation would earn remission of one's need for penance. Prior to Urban II, being a pilgrim generally was associated with contemplation and prayer for penance. This is the world that Francis was born into and that influenced his early life.

It was also a time of theological and philosophical awakening in Western culture. The period from the fall of the Roman Empire until around the tenth century is often mistakenly referred to as the Dark Ages. For Western Europe it was a period of cultural decline and constant war. During this period a lot of classical Greek texts, the works of Aristotle and Plato among others, were lost to the Western world. By St. Francis's time this had changed. The works of Aristotle and Plato were being translated into Latin and Arabic and more readily available to Western Christian thinkers. Ironically it was the work of Muslim scholars in the tenth and eleventh centuries that greatly influenced Christian thought.

The church, at the time of St. Francis, was experiencing the tension of the hierarchical political leadership proclaiming Muslims as the evil spawn of Satan and declaring war on them while theological, philosophical, and scientific leaders were embracing and incorporating the works of earlier Muslim scholars such as Ibn Rushd and Ibn Sina, who were instrumental in saving, translating, and interpreting the works of Aristotle. St. Thomas Aquinas, considered the leading Catholic theologian and proclaimed by Pope Pius V as a doctor of the church in 1567, was strongly influenced by the writings on Aristotle by the eleventh-century Muslim mystic and philosopher Ibn Sina, or as he is commonly known, Avicenna. In all probability, Francis, as a seeker of truth, would have experienced and understood this tension.

Some 640 years later, Charles de Foucauld followed a similar path on his spiritual journey. Foucauld was born in 1858 in Strasburg to aristocratic parents. Six years later both his parents died, and he was placed in the custody of his maternal grandfather. While he was raised Catholic and attended Jesuit schools, by his own admission he lost his faith by age 16. Like St. Francis before him, he was not a serious student and spent his youth frolicking and dreaming of becoming a military hero. In 1876 he entered a military academy, where he was more interested in the parties than the academics. He lasted only two years and was dismissed. A few years later his grandfather died, and Foucauld inherited a considerable amount of money, which he soon squandered. In 1878 he re-entered military school, where in 1879 he graduated, finishing last in his class. In 1880 Foucauld's regiment was sent to Algeria. Algeria at this time was a French colony with a majority Muslim population. In 1881 he went with his regiment to fight in a conflict in Tunisia. It was at this point in time that Foucauld began to develop both a curiosity and respect for the Muslim and Arab world. He later wrote in a letter: "The encounter with Islam caused a profound upheaval within me. . . ."

His curiosity led him to resign from the army and begin a year-long scientific pilgrimage through Morocco. At the time it was forbidden for Christians to enter Morocco, so Foucauld disguised himself as a Jewish Rabbi, Mardochée Aby Serour. Rabbi Mardochée was a well-known explorer and was respected in both the Jewish and Muslim communities. As a result, in addition to his scientific exploration, Foucauld encountered and was able to spend time with the Muslim communities. He published a journal of his Moroccan expedition for which he received a gold medal. What started for Foucauld as a scientific expedition evolved into a spiritual journey—in the same way as when St. Francis returned from war and spent several months wandering around the hillside surrounding Assisi searching for inner peace and meaning. Their encounter with "the other" helped ignite a transformative process that led to a much deeper and fuller relationship with God.

At this point Foucauld was spiritually restless. During his time spent in Morocco and Algeria he began to develop friendships with both Jewish and Muslim folks. He began to understand and appreciate their strong connection to God and each other. Foucauld would often repeat the prayer "*My God, if you exist, make me know you.*" He began attending the Church of St. Augustine in Paris, where Father Henri Huvelin was the pastor. Huvelin was a well-known confessor and spiritual advisor. Foucauld reached out to Huvelin, who took Foucauld under his wing and became his friend. Under Huvelin's guidance, Foucauld joined the Trappists, but he left before taking his final vows. He became somewhat disenchanted. He wanted, like St. Francis, to live with the poorest among the poor, something he accomplished in his last years when he returned to live in Algeria as a hermit among the Tuaregs in the Sahara.

The spirituality of both St. Francis and Foucauld was shaped by their understanding and reflection around the Incarnation. During Francis's time the Incarnation was not considered a central aspect of God's salvific mission. Instead, the prevalent theology of this period centered on the idea of substitutionary atonement. Jesus came as a sacrifice to atone for original sin. The focus was on sin and fallen man. The Incarnation and life

of Jesus were irrelevant. The only important point was the cru-
cifixion. That theology was only strengthened by Thomas Aquinas. But St. Francis and Franciscan theologians saw it differently.
St. Francis was in awe of the concept that God became man.
He understood this as the ultimate gesture of love. In her book
Franciscan Prayer, Sr. Ilia Delio, OSF, expresses Saint Francis's
spiritual aspiration in the following way: "[Franciscan prayer]
. . . begins and ends with the Incarnation. It begins with encountering the God of overflowing love in the person of Jesus Christ
and ends with embodying that love in one's own life, becoming
a new Incarnation. . . . To live the gospel life is to proclaim by
one's life the Good News of God among us and thus to make
Jesus Christ live anew. . . . Incarnation is what all of creation
is about because it is the Word of God made flesh." The bril-
liant thirteenth-century Franciscan theologian and philosopher
Blessed John Dun Scotus wrote: "The Incarnation of the Son of
God is the very reason for the whole Creation. To think that God
would have given up such a task had Adam not sinned would
be quite unreasonable! I say, therefore, that the fall was not the
cause of Christ's predestination and that if no one had fallen,
neither the angel nor man in this hypothesis, Christ would still
have been predestined in the same way." For St. Francis and as
reflected in Franciscan theology, the Incarnation of God's love
was the reason for creation and could not have been an event
that was initiated by sin.

Foucauld wanted to imitate the life of St. Francis. He would
have been very aware of St. Francis's belief and the Franciscan
theology around the Incarnation. Foucauld came to understand, as St. Francis did, the beauty and joy of Christ's presence
in the universe. God's presence came to unite us, through the
Incarnation, in love with all of creation. Foucauld wrote: "The
Incarnation has its source in the goodness of God, but the most
wonderful of all, is the infinite humility that this mystery con-
tains." They both were formed by the understanding that God
didn't need to create, but that God created out of love. Creation
is an act of love. Therefore, as both men understood, our every

action should be an act of love. As the covenant of Noah teaches, this was not just about God loving us and we in turn loving God back, but a covenant between God and all creation. St. Francis and Foucauld both believed that the Incarnation was not about sin but rather about entering into a relationship of love with all creation.

Both men had been spiritually and emotionally wounded as young adults. But their journeys led them to a deeper understanding of their relationship with God. They were both deeply moved and changed by their encounter with Muslims. While it is probable that they both initially set out to convert Muslims, they did so with an understanding and belief that conversion and transformation were not so much the effect of preaching the Gospel than of living the Gospel. Francis is credited with saying we should preach the Gospel at all times—and use words "when necessary." Foucauld, writing in his notes after a retreat in 1897, said: "It is part of your vocation to proclaim the Gospel from the rooftops, not by what you say, but by how you live." They both understood that it was only through relationship, through encounter, listening and dialogue that we can bring about the common good. Their encounters with Islam led both men to understand a view of humanity that did not differentiate along religious beliefs.

Both men were seekers, not content with the status quo but wanting to imagine a world of interconnectedness, a world where we did not see creation as 'other' but as brother. Their encounters with Muslims led both to the strengthening of their Catholic faith. While Francis's encounter with the Sultan Al-Kamal is well known, it was not his first attempt at reaching out to the Muslim community. In the late spring of 1212, he set out for the Holy Land to preach to the Muslims but was shipwrecked off the coast of the Adriatic Sea and had to return. A few years later Francis again set off to seek out Muslims, but he got sick and had to abandon his journey. So Francis would have had at least a rudimentary understanding of Islam when he met the sultan. The Sultan Al-Kamal also had a reputation for being a seeker of truth. He would often invite spiritual mystics and scholars of different faiths to his court. In particular he would often meet with Sufi shaykhs. One such scholar would have been Shams-i Tabrīzī, a Sufi mystic who later became the teacher and guide for Rumi. He was reported to be at the court of the sultan at the same time as St. Francis.

Foucauld may also have been somewhat influenced by Sufi mysticism. His close friend Louis Massignon was heavily inspired by the work of the tenth-century Sufi leader Husayn Ibn Mansur al-Hallaj. Al-Hallaj taught that to find God you had to look inside yourself and others. Massignon spent a significant amount of time researching al-Hallaj and was initially writing his dissertation on him. So it is most likely that Massignon would have discussed with Foucauld both Sufism generally and specifically al-Hallaj. Foucauld in his encounter and understanding of Islam would have most certainly included Sufi mysticism.

We often think of transformation as a onetime event. We have the "aha" moment, see the burning bush, and are transformed. We then can continue our lives as saved holy people praying and worshiping, content in the knowledge that when we die we will go to heaven. But the lives of people like St. Charles de Foucauld and St. Francis teach us that transformation is rarely a one-off event but rather a spiritual journey—a journey in which, through self-reflection and action, we constantly challenge our beliefs; a journey that is less about how we pray or what we believe but rather how we live our lives each and every day.

Though separated by around 640 years St. Francis and Charles de Foucauld were connected by their understanding of completely letting go, both spiritually and materially. St. Francis was once asked if he intended to get married, and he responded that he already had a bride in Lady Poverty. They both knew that in order to completely participate in God's love they had to abandon everything. So it is fitting to close with both the prayer of abandonment by St. Charles de Foucauld and a prayer that St. Francis often prayed.

Charles de Foucauld's
Prayer of Abandonment

Father, I put myself in your hands;
Father, I abandon myself to you.
I entrust myself to you.
Father, do with me as it pleases you.
Whatever you do with me,
I will thank you for it.
Giving thanks for anything, I am ready for anything.
As long as your will, O God, is done in me,
as long as your will is done in all your creatures,
I ask for nothing else, O God.
I put my soul into your hands.
I give it to you, O God,
with all the love of my heart,
because I love you,
and because my love requires me to give myself,
I put myself unreservedly in your hands
with infinite confidence,
because you are my Father.

St. Francis Prayer

Let us desire nothing else
let us wish for nothing else
let nothing else please us and cause us delight
except our Creator and Redeemer and Savior,
the One True God, Who is the Fullness of Good,
all good, every good, the true and supreme Good.
Let nothing hinder us,
nothing separate us or nothing come between us.
"May the power of your love O Lord, fiery and sweet
    as honey,
wean my heart from all that is under heaven,
so that I may die for love of your love,
You who were so good as to die for love of my love.
Amen."

9

United with Jesus Christ in Silence: Spirituality of the Little Brothers of Jesus

Cyril Antony, SJ

In 1996, when I was serving as the director of Vaigarai Publishing House in Dindigul, in Tamil Nadu, a request came from the Alampondi community of the Little Brothers of Jesus to bring out a book on the life of Brother Charles de Foucauld (d. 1916) in Tamil to commemorate the 80th anniversary of his death. We joyfully accepted their request and published it.

Although this book was primarily about the life of Brother Charles, we included the life-experiences of some of the Little Brothers. To know their way of life, I visited and interviewed them in person at Alampondi, Thiruvanamalai district, Tamil Nadu. It was a unique and highly memorable experience for me. The life and mission of the brothers I met there inspired me deeply. I began sharing about the life and mission of Brother Charles and his charism and also about the Little Brothers of Alampondi while giving talks and retreats.

In May 2020, as I was sharing about the life of the Little Brothers and the charism of Brother Charles with Father Victor Edwin SJ over the phone, he requested me to write about my experiences with the Little Brothers at Alampondi for *Salam* magazine—for its special issue on Charles's sainthood. This was a great opportunity to share my experiences and perceptions about the followers of Brother Charles.

One remarkable aspect of the Little Brothers at Alampondi village was their simple way of life, from which their mission sprouted. Their very way of life was their message, not only for the people from different religious and caste backgrounds of the village but also for people living in the vicinity of the village.

Three pioneer missionary brothers, Brother Shanthi from Belgium, Brother Arul and Brother Michael from France, landed in Alampondi in 1964, and this was the beginning of the community of Little Brothers there. Local people donated a housing plot, and the brothers built a house with the help of the people. It was a small house, like any other house in that village.

The brothers' way of life reflected the lifestyle of Jesus of Nazareth—an unassuming lifestyle. Living a Nazarene community life means to live as one among the people. Through their work, the brothers were deeply rooted in the lives of the people. The kind of work they chose in order to get inserted in the lives of people involved working in homes for the aged, for mentally and physically challenged children, schools for dropout children, HIV-AIDS centers, etc.

Charles felt that his call was to go to the "lost sheep," to the most abandoned, the most needy, so as to fulfill the commandment of love toward them, to live with the lost and the last. The core spirituality of Charles is to live the life of Nazareth. What does "Nazareth" mean? "Nazareth" means God is always with you in your life! The "Way of Unity," our spiritual road map, speaks to us of the spirituality of "Nazareth." At Nazareth the mystery of God is revealed. Brother Charles was always very captivated by the mystery of Nazareth and by the hidden life that Jesus lived there during the first thirty years of his life.

"Nazareth" is not a dogma but a living model that is possible for each person. To explain what "Nazareth" means, one can reply: "A simple, unassuming life in the midst of the world which can be lived anywhere."

"Nazareth" means living relationships in a brotherly and sisterly way in a spirit of service and simplicity, accepting one's own limitations as well as those of others. It is to meet people without prejudice, to value one another, and to give a positive self-image to all. It is a choice of a simple and shared lifestyle. Friendship reveals God in our own lives and helps us to become, more and more, universal brothers and sisters. "Nazareth" is to live events of ordinary life as extraordinary.

"Like Jesus, you will eat with your brothers and sisters and you will rejoice with them. You will accept their hospitality with simplicity, living your Christian and religious life among them in a sisterly and brotherly way, so as to show them its beauty and greatness," said one of the brothers. He added: "Our vocation in the church is to be a reminder of the mystery of Bethlehem and the hidden life of Jesus in Nazareth."

In line with the way of life they choose to lead, the Little Brothers should not employ any workers in their house. And, they themselves must be employed outside. Brother Shanthi was employed in a nearby private leprosy hospital; Brother Arul did farm work as a daily laborer; Brother Michael prepared naturopathy medicines, particularly for diabetes, which he would give to people in and around Alampondi. Using their meager income, they maintained their life. They did all kinds of housework, such as cooking, cleaning, purchasing, etc., by themselves.

The dynamic presence of the positive example of a person can help make other people's life and mission meaningful and fruitful. Brother Charles is still remembered by many people and inspires them because of his dynamic, committed, and humble way of life. He sincerely searched and lived the life of consecrated life—witnessing to God and the world.

Being intimately united with Jesus Christ in silence, to be with the people, especially the marginalized, having a simple and hidden way of life, and respecting people of other faiths were some fundamental principles that Charles left behind, which we can greatly benefit from.

Blessed Charles was the inspiration for the founding of several lay associations, religious communities, and secular institutes of laity and priests, known collectively as "the spiritual family of Charles de Foucauld."

Hospitality is an important human value that Little Brothers try to put into practice. They are happy in sharing what they have. I experienced this at Alampondi. In Bangalore, where the brothers have a community, people love to visit the brothers' house because they show love and compassion. Their joyful living has helped build a good rapport with people from different faith backgrounds.

Community life is an important area where the brothers show their love for one another. There is a family spirit among them. Since their congregation does not run institutions, they do not fight for the power and position. Rather, they serve others, including one another. I could see joy and happiness in the faces of the brothers when I met them at Alampondi.

Making friendship with people is yet another strong value that the brothers follow in their life. At Alampondi, the brothers enjoyed a strong loving relationship with the local people. Their relationship with the people gave them a sense of belonging. Charles discovered that Jesus invites us to that universal brotherhood.

In principle, the brothers do not get ordained, although they undergo formal theological studies. However, for their spiritual needs, they select one or two brothers to get ordained. They help the nearby parishes, but their focus is to be with the people, including people of other faiths.

At present, the brothers live in 38 countries, and they number 270 in all. In India, they have two communities, in Bangalore and in Thiruvannamalai, with a total of six brothers.

The life of Brother Charles and his followers challenges present-day Christian religious life and mission. More institutions, lack of brotherly love, care, and concern, distancing from the life-situations of the people, aspiring for more power and position, etc. make many religious in different Christian congregations alienated from the spirit and vision of their founders.

The brothers' life is very hard. Some young people come and live with them for a few weeks and then most of them leave. Hardly a few remain. This is the universal experience of the brothers all over the world. But the brothers unanimously feel that they want to continue their rigorous way of life. Even though the number is just six in India and 270 globally, they are not disappointed. Rather, they are hopeful.

Anyone can join the congregation of the brothers, even those who have minimal educational qualifications. Educational qualification is not the main criteria to decide anyone's vocation. Rather, it is the spirit, enthusiasm, commitment, and sense of mission that make one's vocation truthful and meaningful.

For the brothers, formation is not given within the four walls of a classroom, with a pre-determined number of formal classes. Rather, their formation happens while sharing in the lives of the people and in the course of leading a simple way of life. Unlike other congregations, they do not have formation houses. Rather, among the brothers there is one who is in charge of the young brothers.

The brothers depend on God's providence. All the brothers I met at Alampondi said that they had never experienced not having food, money, and other basic necessities. Brother Charles insisted that the brothers should live with the poor and that their residence must be like poor people's homes. They should accept the life of the poor and live like them.

In India, few Christian youth showed interest in joining the congregation of Little Brothers, and also the Little Sisters. Was it because of the tough way of life of the brothers, and the sisters? Or because they do not have even a single educational institution, where some people can find security and comfort?

The lifestyle of Charles is tough, but of more witnessing value. Brother Charles adopted a new apostolic approach, preaching not through sermons, but through his personal example. Charles wanted to "shout the Gospel with his life" and to conduct his life in such a way that people would ask, "If such is the servant, what must the Master be like?"

The spirituality of universal love and brotherhood of Charles gives hope to a new world. A new way of life is possible when people are loved. Love is the greatest power in the world. It can change everything.

Above all, we must always see Jesus in every person, and, consequently, treat each person as an equal and as a brother or sister, and with great humility, respect and selfless generosity.

10

My Journey with
St. Charles de Foucauld

Joseph G. Healey, MM

A JOURNEY TIMELINE

January 1960, Glen Ellyn, Illinois, USA

I was introduced to Brother Charles de Foucauld during our philosophy studies at the Maryknoll Seminary in Glen Ellyn. He was held up as a special missionary model of prayer and presence in North Africa. The principal task of the churches in North Africa, their activity of evangelization, is only possible with a fruitful presence of silence, prayer, contemplation, and suffering. This is the model of evangelization inaugurated by Charles, who lived for years in Tamanrasset in Algeria in the solitude of the desert, made fruitful by the contemplation of God present in the mystery of the Eucharist.

We had long discussions on the meaning of presence, especially spiritual presence. Charles was different from missionaries like St. Paul and St. Francis Xavier, who achieved so much in the preaching and teaching aspects of their mission. I remember St. Teresa of Calcutta saying: "God does not ask us to be successful, but to be faithful." The Jewish philosopher and theologian Martin Buber has said that "success is not one of the names of God."

January 1962, Bedford, Massachusetts, USA

I read *The Sands of Tamanrasset: The Story of Charles de Foucauld* by Marion Mill Preminger and some writings of René Voillaume during our Maryknoll novitiate. Later on, books that had an influence on me included the Orbis Books *Letters from the Desert* by Carlo Carretto, a Little Brother of the Gospel, and *Charles de Foucauld* (Modern Spiritual Masters). We are grateful that so many followers of Brother Charles have chronicled their inspiring spiritual journeys.

November 1967, Maryknoll, New York, USA

My journey with Brother Charles really began when I joined a Jesus Caritas Fraternity at the Maryknoll Seminary in New York. It was a small group of Maryknoll priests on stateside assignments. The "Review of Life"[1] was a special feature of our little community. We also scheduled special "Desert Days."

July 1972, Kajiado, Kenya

I made a private retreat near the Fraternity of the Little Sisters of Jesus in Kajiado, Kenya. In my prayer and discernment inspired by Brother Charles I felt called to live a ministry of spiritual presence in my Maryknoll missionary vocation. This would mean living a more contemplative life and a deeper sharing in the life of the poor and simple people on the local level in Tanzania.

---

1. The "Review of Life" is a prayer experience of deep sharing and discernment that can be described as praying in a synodal way where everyone is walking together and helping each other. Parallel practices include the Jesuit method of prayer called the Daily Examen, or examination of conscience, or what in the Small Christian Communities we sometimes call the sharing of "God moments," when each member tells of a time he or she has experienced God during the week. This is documented in Joseph Healey, *Building the Church as Family of God: Evaluation of Small Christian Communities in Eastern Africa*, online ebook, on the Small Christian Communities Global Collaborative Website: https://smallchristian communities.org/building-the-church-as-family-of-god-evaluation-of-small-christian-communities-in-eastern-africa-2/.

December 1974, Israel

During a pilgrimage to the Holy Land I spent several days in Nazareth meditating on the "Hidden Life of Nazareth," so loved by Brother Charles. My spiritual journal reads:

> It is important to recall that Jesus Christ lived 30 of his 33 years here in Nazareth—silent years of growth and preparation. But we know so little about these 30 years. Certainly Jesus grew up in a happy home where religion and dedicated work played a big part. I am reminded of a beautiful prayer calling on Mary and Joseph for guidance and help: "Just as you were beside Jesus, you are beside us to accompany us to eternal life, to teach us to be small and poor in our work, humble and hidden in life, courageous in trial, faithful in prayer, ardent in love."

My journal continues:

> I celebrated mass in the old Poor Clare Convent now occupied in part by the Little Sisters of Charles de Foucauld. In this chapel Brother Charles spent many hours in prayer during the three years (1897–1900) that he worked as a gardener for the Poor Clares. The mass was in English, French, and Arabic.
>
> Two hours of meditation and reflection bring new thoughts and feelings. Charles de Foucauld tried in a very special way to imitate the life of Jesus at Nazareth—a life of prayer, poverty, humility, and physical labor. "Contemplation in the world" is the way the Little Brothers and Little Sisters of Jesus describe their hidden life of imitating Jesus Christ at Nazareth.
>
> I met the Little Brothers and Little Sisters at different places in the Holy Land—Afula, Bethlehem, Jerusalem, and Nazareth. They really live a contemplative state of life in the midst of the world—imitating Jesus's hidden years as much as possible. Working as a metal worker in a factory, making ceramics, mending clothes, running a

small dispensary—such is their work in the Holy Land today as Jesus worked as a carpenter in Nazareth 2,000 years ago.

One Little Brother has built a little retreat place—a hermitage—on the top of the Mount of Beatitudes in Galilee. Built out of thousands of rocks and stones that cover the mountain, the hermitage is a place of prayer and meditation. Just as Jesus went off alone to pray, men and women follow in his steps today.

I discovered Charles's *Journal*, which has detailed reflections on Mary and Joseph's day-by-day travel on foot from Nazareth to Bethlehem before the birth of Jesus Christ. His reflections are poignant and inspiring. I have tried to read these reflections yearly ever since.

September 1976, Nyabihanga, Tanzania

I began living in an *Ujamaa* (Swahili for familyhood) village in Rulenge Diocese in Western Tanzania with two Little Brothers of Jesus—Marcel Jagu from France and Fabian Ntubwa from the Democratic Republic of the Congo (DRC). I shared the life of the simple Tanzanian farmers and promoted the Small Christian Community model of church.[2] Our inspiration was Bishop Christopher Mwoleka, the Catholic Bishop of Rulenge, who joined us from time to time.

October 1982, Musoma, Tanzania

I joined the Jesus Caritas Fraternity in Musoma Diocese in Tanzania. We were Maryknoll priests and American diocesan priests serving in mission with Maryknoll (Maryknoll Priest Associates). Our simple program: "Review of Life." Mass. Adoration of the Blessed Sacrament. Socializing. Gradually we became a bonded community.

---

2. See Joseph Healey and Jeanne Hinton, eds., *Small Christian Communities Today: Capturing the New Moment* (Maryknoll, NY: Orbis Books, 2005; Nairobi: Paulines Publications Africa, 2006).

I liked the "Review of Life" best. Each priest would share a concrete experience since we had last gathered. We would look for common features. Then we would go in depth in reflecting on one experience. Over the years many similar themes arose, including issues around acculturation. At virtually every meeting one of us would bring up a specific instance or culturally related challenge that was cause for personal frustration, and most everyone would readily identify with it. We discussed how to deal with transitions in missionary life—whether returning to the United States, or accepting new mission assignments. We also talked about how to make prayer and contemplation a more important part of our busy missionary ministry, and how to better relate to the Tanzanian people and their needs.

Our "Review of Life" was very prayerful. It was not a problem-solving exercise nor a counseling session. Rather it was deep listening, a kind of community discernment and a type of community spiritual direction. We would have several rounds of reflecting on the themes/questions and always trying to go deeper.

July 1991, Denver, Colorado

Month of Nazareth. To celebrate my 25th anniversary of Maryknoll Missionary Priesthood I joined two African diocesan priests and priests from the United States for four weeks together. As described in the *Directory*: "The Month of Nazareth is a sharing of the fraternal life at every level: prayer, reflection, manual work, leisure, etc. There is a deepening shared spiritual awareness of the great original intuitions of the Fraternity, with an attempt to confront the conflicting appeals of the Catholic Church and the world, the situations in which priests have to live." Conflicting appeals today might be the persuasive power of the internet and smartphone and the lure of the secular world.

November 1994

I was assigned to the Maryknoll Society House in Dar es Salaam, Tanzania. I could not find a Jesus Caritas Fraternity of priests.

So I joined a Jesus Caritas Fraternity of laymen and laywomen. There is a saying, "When God closes a door somewhere he opens a window." I was inspired by the dedication of these laypeople and their commitment to Jesus Caritas spirituality.

January 2020, Nairobi, Kenya

At 81–years-old I am in a three-year transition period of handing over my missionary ministries to members of the local church in Eastern Africa. A one-hour meditation on Charles de Foucauld's "Hidden life of Nazareth" ended with the Gospel mantra: "He must increase; I must decrease" (John 3:30). This applies to Maryknollers like myself handing over our ministries to the local church and moving on—with the humility, hiddenness, and littleness that this requires.

August 2021, New Vernon, New Jersey, USA

Due to the Covid-19 pandemic, I am temporarily living at my brother's home in New Jersey—waiting for the Delta variant to cool down before returning to Nairobi, Kenya. While I do not belong to a specific Jesus Caritas Fraternity right now, I am trying to adjust and adapt to today's reality and the local context. A "given" is a one hour "Meditation" every Saturday morning when I combine a personal "Review of Life" with a "Conversation with Jesus Christ" based on the story of the "Two Disciples on the Road to Emmaus." This is followed by a half hour of "Quiet" or "Centering Prayer" when I imagine myself in Brother Charles's chapel in his hermitage in Tamanrasset praying before the Blessed Sacrament. I use a simple Jesus Prayer and visually focus on the host in the monstrance to ward off distractions.

MISSIONARY REFLECTIONS

These missionary reflections have emerged from a lifetime of keeping a spiritual journal.

1. I am a Maryknoll missionary priest who has been ordained for 55 years. My missionary ministry has been deeply influenced

by Jesus's words: "Let us go on to the next towns that I may preach there also; for this purpose have I come" (Mark 1:38).

I used this passage in my homily at my 50th anniversary of Maryknoll Missionary Priesthood (Golden Jubilee) Mass at the Maryknoll Society House in Nairobi on January 14, 2016. I shared that the new "town or place" for me is not a physical or geographical place, but a virtual or existential or situational place: the internet, social media, and social networking. So mission for me means going to the "towns" of Zoom, Facebook, Instagram, Skype, YouTube and WhatsApp. I mentioned that I meet and interact with Kenyan young people not outside the church after the Sunday Mass but in the social media on the internet.

2. This life of a missionary means that I am always on the move and do not have a permanent living community. So I have been in a variety of Jesus Caritas Fraternities over the years. But the fixed points have been sharing and discerning with Reflection Partners on our Jesus Caritas spirituality, trying to live this in different conscious ways. Brother Charles is a model for identifying with the poor and needy. This connects very well with Pope Francis's challenge today to "reach out to the marginated and those on the periphery of society."

3. The quotation of Brother Charles that I have used the most over many years is: "If you can suffer and love you can do anything, even things that are impossible."

Charles understood suffering in two ways. First is personal suffering. This can be physical, emotional, psychological, and spiritual. We have the perfect physical model in Jesus's way of the cross and death on the cross. As Rick Dixon, a former Little Brother of the Gospel and a returned Maryknoll Lay Missioner from El Salvador, adds: "When Brother Charles lived with the Tuareg Ethnic Group in Algeria and he fell ill, the desert nomads took him in and nourished him with their precious goat milk which he realized should have been going to their children. Spiritual presence took on a humbling new meaning, a two-way accompaniment. What a powerful lesson in solidarity and abandonment into the hands of God, into the hands of the Tuareg."

Second is suffering with the poorest and neediest and sharing the suffering of the world. It means deeper listening, identification with, solidarity with, empathy with and accompanying suffering people either in one's family, neighborhood, or around the world—victims of war in Afghanistan, earthquakes in Haiti, and refugees in North Africa. I know people who whenever they hear the siren of an ambulance pray for and with the sick person. Other people remember refugees (who are endlessly walking) as they walk up and down stairs. Other people travel in economy class on planes and trains remembering Charles's words: "I do not want to travel through life first class when the One that I love went in the lowest class." Charles adds: "I want to live in a small monastery, like the house of a poor workman who is not sure if tomorrow he will find work and bread, who with all his being shares the suffering of the world."

Another solidarity example. Some of us expatriate missionaries living in Africa get up very early—sometimes at three a.m. and four a.m. I begin my day with prayer, meditation, and writing. I can do this wherever I am. Inspired by Brother Charles every day at this very early time we are in solidarity with African farmers who get up very early and have to walk one to two hours in the dark to their fields and African city workers who get up very early and board buses for one- to two-hour trips, even three hours in bad weather, to their downtown jobs.

4. I knew the Little Sisters of Jesus and the Little Sisters of the Gospel when I was living in Nairobi, Kenya. I don't think I have ever met any religious group of women or men who lived more simply or were so joyful. I visited their simple hermitage in Kajiado, Kenya. Their hospitality, joy, and sharing helped me to appreciate Charles and his spirituality more. I remember reading a survey of religious sisters around the world. I don't remember who was rated the happiest group, but the Little Sisters, an international congregation, came in second! The reason: they have learned to live with one another's temperaments.

5. For many years I have struggled with Charles de Foucauld's "Prayer of Abandonment." The "all" or "total commitment" of the words of the prayer was always too much for me. As I said this prayer, mainly in a small community setting, I just didn't feel right. I was saying "words" without living their deeper meaning. Then during a retreat I got the insight that I was trying too hard. To understand the deeper, heart meaning of this prayer, I realized that the key was to "try" to abandon myself to God, to "make the effort" to abandon myself to God. Then leave the success part to God. So now I pray the "Prayer of Abandonment" as a "prayer in progress."

6. Another spiritual connection is the close link between St. Charles de Foucauld and St. Thérèse of Lisieux. First, let us reflect on Charles. A lot has been written on Marie de Bondy, Charles's cousin in France, with whom he had a deep spiritual relationship. They were like spiritual brother and sister. Her friendship, advice, and rich correspondence were a great support to Charles during his lifetime spiritual journey and search and his eventual life of spiritual presence in North Africa.

Then let us reflect on Thérèse, who is the Patroness of Mission and a Patroness of the Maryknoll Society of Priests and Brothers. The Carmelite nuns have a tradition of praying for and with missionaries. This includes developing spiritual-sister/missionary-brother relationships. As a Carmelite sister living in France, Thérèse had two missionary brothers, one a French Missionary of Africa (formerly the White Fathers) who served in Malawi. I am blessed to have a spiritual sister—Sister Colette Ackerman, OCD, of the Carmelite Monastery in Baltimore, Maryland, USA—since before I was ordained in 1966. She has been a close companion on the "journey," and we have shared many of the missionary reflections in this essay.

We see how close is the spirituality of Charles and Thérèse—abandonment to God, denying God nothing, handing over our will to God, loving fully always and to the end, contemplation, littleness, hiddenness, simplicity, poverty, and the hermitic life. Marie de Bondy sent Thérèse's autobiography *The Story of a*

Soul to Charles in his hermitage in Algeria. We know that he received the parcel, but unfortunately we have never heard about Charles's reactions. But for sure, Charles's "Hidden Life of Nazareth" is very close to Thérèse's "Little Way of Spiritual Childhood." I had a similar reaction when the Catholic Church wanted to make Thérèse a doctor of the church and Charles a saint. I deeply felt that given their spirituality of littleness and hiddenness, they wouldn't have wanted these public honors. But it was clearly the *sensus fidelium*, the popular voice of the people. In some paradoxical way these honors and this recognition give special value to their littleness and hiddenness.

7. A clear sign of the times is how Pope Francis in the encyclical *Fratelli tutti* (2020) draws inspiration from Blessed [now Saint] Charles de Foucauld:

> In these pages of reflection on universal fraternity, I felt inspired particularly by Saint Francis of Assisi, but also by others of our brothers and sisters who are not Catholics: Martin Luther King, Desmond Tutu, Mahatma Gandhi and many more. Yet I would like to conclude by mentioning another person of deep faith who, drawing upon his intense experience of God, made a journey of transformation toward feeling a brother to all. I am speaking of Blessed [now Saint] Charles de Foucauld. (286)
>
> Blessed [now Saint] Charles directed his ideal of total surrender to God toward an identification with the poor, abandoned in the depths of the African desert. In that setting, he expressed his desire to feel himself a brother to every human being, and asked a friend to "pray to God that I truly be the brother of all." He wanted to be, in the end, "the universal brother." Yet only by identifying with the least did he come at last to be the brother of all. May God inspire that dream in each one of us. Amen. (287)

THE WAY FORWARD

The canonization of St. Charles de Foucauld on May 15, 2022, begins a new chapter in the Catholic Church in the world as we read the contemporary signs of the times. I even feel the several postponements of his canonization due to the Covid-19 pandemic had a special message for us. Brother Charles (as I am sure he would still want us to refer to him) calls us to a life and ministry of spiritual presence. This has many implications for some of the burning questions of our times: How do we live out Jesus Christ's words that "whatever you do to the least of these brothers and sisters you do to me"? How do we engage in interreligious dialogue, especially with Muslims? How are we to be universal brothers and sisters in today's world? How do we respond to the many kinds of poverty in the world today, including spiritual poverty as well as material poverty? How do we engage in evangelization in North Africa? How do we pursue the ministry of deeper listening and accompaniment so dear to the heart of Pope Francis? As the Spanish proverb says: *We create the path by walking.*

11

The "Universal Brother" St. Charles de Foucauld: His Life and Relevance Today

Rita George-Tvrtković, PhD

Blessed Charles directed his ideal of total surrender to God towards an identification with the poor, abandoned in the depths of the African desert. In that setting, he expressed his desire to feel himself a brother to every human being, and asked a friend to "pray to God that I truly be the brother of all." He wanted to be, in the end, "the universal brother." Yet only by identifying with the least did he come at last to be the brother of all.

—Pope Francis, *Fratelli tutti*

In the very last lines of Pope Francis's newest encyclical *Fratelli tutti*, just released in October 2020, the Holy Father holds up Blessed Charles de Foucauld (d. 1916) as a model of universal brotherhood. And now, since May 2022, he has been declared a canonized saint. So who was Charles de Foucauld and why does his life matter today?

HIS LIFE

Vicomte (Viscount) Charles-Eugène de Foucauld was born on September 15, 1858, in Strasbourg, France. He came from a noble, wealthy, ancient family, whose lineage can be traced as far back as the tenth century; ancestors included Crusaders, royal consorts, churchmen, and philanthropists. His family's prominence is evident by the very existence of a photograph of young Charles with his mother, Élisabeth de Morlet, and baby sister, Marie, circa 1863, at a time when few could afford a portrait in the new medium of photography. It was not long after the photo was taken that Charles, at age six, lost both parents and his grandmother; he and Marie were raised by their grandfather. By the age of 22, Foucauld had left the Catholic faith, been expelled from a Jesuit school, squandered much of the family fortune he inherited, finished last in his class at a military academy, joined the French army, and took his mistress with him on a military expedition to Algeria and Tunisia.

While in North Africa, he became enthralled with the beauty of the land and was touched by the piety of local Muslims. He wanted to visit Morocco, but the country prohibited European visitors at the time, so he disguised himself as a Moroccan Jew, calling himself "Rabbi Joseph." He eventually traveled over three thousand kilometers in a country largely unknown to Europeans, secretly keeping a journal and surveying the land as he went; for this, he received a gold medal from the French Geographic Society. When he returned to Paris and published his journal and surveys in a book, *Reconnaissance au Maroc*, he became somewhat famous. But Foucauld did not care about fame or fortune; instead, he started to pray and reminisce about his humble North African journey, which he considered a kind of pilgrimage. He also began to contemplate entering religious life.

Foucauld joined the Trappists in 1890 but soon thirsted for an even more austere lifestyle. After just seven years, he left the Trappists and went to Nazareth, where he lived as a hermit in a tool shed and did manual labor for the Poor Clares who hosted him. It was in Nazareth that he began to write his "Rule for Little Brothers." After moving back to France and being ordained a priest, he realized that his vocation was to live among the most needy, the people he called the "lost sheep": the Muslims of North Africa.

Foucauld began his new ministry in earnest at Beni Abbès, a tiny oasis town on the border of Algeria and Morocco. Within a few years, he went even farther afield, to the remote Saharan outpost of Tamanrasset, in southern Algeria, where he set up a hermitage at nearby Assekrem (a three-day camel ride from town) to live among the nomadic Tuareg Muslims. He described his time there as one of prayer and mutual hospitality: the locals welcomed him, and he in turn opened his hermitage to guests of all kinds, at all hours. With Christ's command "whatever you did for the least of my brothers and sisters, you did for me'" (Matthew 25:40) ever in his mind, Foucauld hoped that his Muslim neighbors would see him as their brother. He also hoped other Christians would join him in his new order, which he called "The Fraternity of the Sacred Heart of Jesus." His idea of fraternity was not limited to monks or even to Christians: "I want all inhabitants, be they Christian, Muslim, or Jewish, to look on me as their brother, the universal brother." Perhaps his vision was ahead of its time, for the hermitage was a failure. No one joined. And he gained not a single Muslim convert. After twelve years, some might have wondered about the purpose of his mission. Aside from translating the Gospels into Tuareg, and compiling a Tuareg–French dictionary, what had he accomplished? But to him, this hospitable yet solitary desert life was the most authentic imitation of Christ: he led a simple life among the poor, he prayed and worked (*ora et labora*—the Trappist and Benedictine creed), and most importantly, he lived in harmony with his Muslim neighbors. Locals considered him a marabout (holy man).

On December 1, 1916, Foucauld was killed by Tuaregs from a different village. With his death, it might appear that his vision for a religious order founded on brotherhood had ended. But eventually, Foucauld's idea caught on, in part thanks to the biography by René Bazin, *Charles de Foucauld: Explorateur du Maroc, Ermite au Sahara*, published in 1921. By 1933, Foucauld's successors had founded a new religious order, the Little

Brothers of Jesus, with the Little Sisters of Jesus following soon after in 1939. Today, 19 religious orders, secular institutes, and lay associations trace their roots to Foucauld and his idea of universal fraternity. While the hermit might have died alone in the Algerian wilderness, he eventually birthed a large spiritual family, with many "children" around the world.

HIS RELEVANCE

Today, some have criticized Foucauld as an agent of French colonialism. And indeed, the native of Strasbourg likely would never have traveled to North Africa if not for French colonialism. But Foucauld's supporters emphasize his evolution from desiring to convert his Muslim neighbors to desiring their friendship and fraternity. Foucauld's mission of presence, which he dubbed "doing good in silence," is an approach that would be imitated eight decades later by the French Trappists of Tibhirine, Algeria, who likewise considered their mission one of presence. They too befriended their Muslim neighbors, served them in the local medical clinic, stood by them in solidarity during a bloody civil war, and were killed by extremists in 1996. Since we have access to Charles de Foucauld's desert life only via photographs, watching the film *Des hommes et des dieux* ("Of Gods and Men," 2010), which depicts the affection between the Tibhirine Trappists and their Muslim neighbors, might give us a sense of what Foucauld's life in Algeria was actually like. We know that the abbot of the Tibhirine Trappists, Christian de Chergé, was inspired by Foucauld, having read about him while studying at the Pontifical Institute for Arabic and Islamic Studies (PISAI) in Rome. Chergé even confirmed his religious vocation to live among Muslims by going on a two-month solitary retreat at Foucauld's old hermitage in Assekrem. He expressed this vocation in myriad ways at his Our Lady of Atlas Monastery in northern Algeria; for example, Chergé hung a sign that read "Muslims welcome for retreats here," and co-founded a local interfaith dialogue group. Clearly, Christian and Charles were kindred spirits, following similar life paths. Like Foucauld, Chergé began as a military man in North Africa, as part of the French colonial machine; and yet, both men, by virtue of their long-term spiritual commitment to North Africa and its people, had memorable encounters with holy Muslims who profoundly deepened their own Catholic faith.

But Foucauld was not only influential after his death; he had protégés even during his lifetime. For although he lived alone in his desert hermitage, he maintained a correspondence with friends and colleagues abroad, most notably Louis Massignon (d. 1962). Massignon was a French Catholic scholar of Islam who would go on to teach two key framers of *Nostra Aetate's* section 3 on Islam: the Dominican Georges Anawati and the Missionary of Africa Robert Caspar. Massignon's own spiritual path was deeply influenced by Foucauld, whom he describes in an article devoted entirely to him: "Foucauld was given to me like an older brother and helped me to find my brothers in all human beings, starting with the most abandoned ones."[1] Massignon considered Foucauld to be an extraordinary missionary because he rarely preached but instead "came to share the humble life of the most humble, earning his daily bread with them by the 'holy work of his hands,' before revealing to them, by his silent example, the real spiritual bread of hospitality that these humble people themselves had offered him."[2] Foucauld had such an impact on Massignon that he believed the hermit was one of several intercessors praying for him on the night of his crisis and conversion in 1908. Soon after, Massignon wrote Foucauld a letter of thanks, and they began a correspondence. They finally met in Paris in 1909 and promised to pray for each other daily. After Foucauld's death, Massignon was influential in keeping alive Foucauld's vision of an order devoted to universal brotherhood.

---

1. Louis Massignon, "An Entire Life with a Brother Who Set out on the Desert: Charles de Foucauld," in *Testimonies and Reflections: Essays of Louis Massignon* (ed. and trans. Herbert Mason; Notre Dame, IN: University of Notre Dame Press, 1989), 22.

2. Massignon, "An Entire Life with a Brother," 22–23.

Foucauld also influenced the spirituality of other prominent lay Catholics of the twentieth century, including the American Dorothy Day and the French husband–wife duo Jacques and Raïssa Maritain. In their book *Liturgy and Contemplation*, the Maritains expressed their admiration for the vocation of Foucauld and his Little Brothers: "It seems that constant attention to the presence of Jesus and fraternal charity are called to play a major role . . . we believe that the vocation of those contemplatives thrown into the miseries of the world, the Little Brothers of Charles de Foucauld, has in this respect a high significance."[3] (After the death of Raïssa, Jacques—one of the most eminent Catholic philosophers of his time—actually joined the Little Brothers of Jesus and died in their fraternity in Toulouse.) Dorothy Day, co-founder of the Catholic Worker movement in New York, once participated in a retreat centered on the life of Charles de Foucauld, and explained why she was so inspired by him and the Little Brothers and Sisters: "One of the reasons that I am so strongly attracted to the spirit of this 'family' is of course its emphasis on poverty as a means, poverty as an expression of love, poverty because Jesus lived it. And then too the emphasis on humble manual labor is for all."[4] Thanks to their stress on manual labor and service to the poor, Foucauld's Little Brothers and Sisters also influenced the French worker-priest movement of the 1950s.

Today, communities of Little Brothers and Sisters of Jesus can be found in nearly 90 countries around the world, not only in Charles's beloved Algeria, but also Burkina Faso, Papua New Guinea, Syria, England, Haiti, Canada, Bolivia, India, and Vietnam, just to name a few. And as Charles de Foucauld moves closer to sainthood, more and more lay people are discovering him through popular Catholic literature, such as the collection of Foucauld's writings edited by Robert Ellsberg (Orbis Books, 2005), and the book about him written by a Muslim, *A Christian Hermit in an Islamic World: A Muslim's View of Charles de*

---

3. Jacques and Raïssa Maritain, *Liturgy and Contemplation* (New York: P. J. Kenedy & Sons, 1960), 76.

4. Dorothy Day, "Retreat," *The Catholic Worker*, August 1959, 2, 7, 8.

Foucauld, by Ali Merad (Paulist Press, 2000). Online references to Foucauld abound as well. To cite just one example: Father James Martin, an American Jesuit with 636,000 Facebook followers, posted this in May 2020: "Saint Charles de Foucauld, pray for us! I knew the Little Sisters of Jesus when I was living in Nairobi, Kenya, and I don't think I have ever met any religious group of women or men who lived more simply or were so joyful. Their hospitality and joy led me to a deep devotion to Charles." Today, Charles de Foucauld has wide appeal due to his simplicity, spirituality, and love for the poor. However, he remains most influential among Christians engaged in dialogue with Muslims. As already noted above, Pope Francis has been so taken by Foucauld that he holds him up as a model of fraternity. It seems likely that Francis also sees him as a model of interfaith dialogue too, given that the encyclical's mention of Foucauld directly follows a lengthy description of another example of Christian-Muslim dialogue, that of his own encounters and collaboration with Grand Imam Ahmad al-Tayyeb of Al-Azhar.

Charles de Foucauld was a hermit, manual laborer, lover of the poor, friend to Muslims, and brother of all. Now he is also recognized as a saint. In a 1959 *Catholic Worker* newspaper article about him, Dorothy Day linked his vocation to Christ's, the one whose footsteps he sought to follow when he first moved to Nazareth and then to Algeria. Day's final reflection on Foucauld is thus a good place for this article to end:

> How far one's vocation will take one is always a mystery, and where one's vocation will take one. But I believe it to be true that the foundations are always in poverty, manual labor, and in seeming failure. It is the pattern of the Cross, and in the Cross is joy of spirit.[5]

---

5. Day, "Retreat," 2, 7, 8.

Contributors

Cyril Antony, SJ, is a member of Madurai Jesuit Province and a human rights educator. He served as the director of Vaigarai Publishing House for twelve years at Dindigul. He has been state coordinator for Human Rights Education Programme in schools since 1998. At present he is the director of Gandhian Society Villages Association (GANSOVILLE) at Devakottai, Tamil Nadu (India), advocating Gandhian values and vision.

Patrick Carolan is a Catholic activist, organizer, writer, speaker, and story teller. He served as the executive director of the Franciscan Action Network, co-founded both the Global Catholic Climate Movement and the Faithful Democracy Coalition. He previously was a union organizer and served as president of a state public employee union. Patrick resides in Connecticut, USA, with his wife, Stella. Together they raised four children, two biological and two adopted. They also took care of several other foster children. They try to celebrate God's love by living every day in the kinship of creation.

Joseph Victor Edwin, SJ, is a Jesuit priest who teaches Christian-Muslim Relations at Vidyajyoti, a Catholic centre for higher theological learning in Delhi. He is deeply engaged in seeking to promote understanding and goodwill between Christians and Muslims. He has a PhD in Islamic Studies from Jamia Millia Islamia, New Delhi. His recent publication is *A New Spirit in Christian-Muslim Relations in India: Three Jesuit Pioneers* (New Delhi: ISPCK, 2021).

Rita George-Tvrtković (PhD, University of Notre Dame) is associate professor of theology at Benedictine University in suburban

Chicago, where she specializes in medieval Christian-Muslim relations and the contemporary theology and praxis of inter-religious dialogue. Her books include *A Christian Pilgrim in Medieval Iraq: Riccoldo da Montecroce's Encounter with Islam* (Brepols Publishers, 2012), and *Christians, Muslims, and Mary: A History* (Paulist Press, 2018). Her articles have appeared in *Theological Studies, Catholic Historical Review, Medieval Encounters*, and *America*. A former associate director of the Archdiocese of Chicago's Office for Ecumenical and Interreligious Affairs, she was recently appointed by Pope Francis to be a consultor for the Pontifical Council for Interreligious Dialogue.

Marc Hayet, who was born in the southwest of France, joined the Little Brothers of Jesus fifty years ago. As a Little Brother of Jesus, he has lived in working-class neighborhoods of large cities in France, working in factories and as a cleaning worker. To be a Little Brother of Jesus, Marc feels, is an opportunity to share with the poor, their joys and sorrows, and to walk on a path on which the Risen One walks with us and reveals his presence.

Joseph G. Healey, MM, is an American Maryknoll missionary priest who lives in Nairobi, Kenya. He came to Kenya in 1968 and founded the Regional Catholic Bishops Association (AME-CEA) Social Communications Office based in Nairobi. He is currently a lecturer at Tangaza University College (CUEA) and at Hekima University College (CUEA) in Nairobi. He is a member of the AMECEA Small Christian Communities (SCCs) Training Team and facilitates SCC Workshops in Eastern Africa. During the Covid-19 pandemic he has focused on a new ministry: promoting online SCCs. He is the author of *Towards an African Narrative Theology* (Orbis Books, 1997) and *Small Christian Communities Today* (Orbis Books, 2005).

Little Sister Kathleen joined the Little Sisters of Jesus in Montreal in 1981. For ten years she was a member of the community's formation team in Rome before being sent to Walsingham, England.

Christian Krokus is professor of theology/religious studies at the University of Scranton, Pennsylvania, USA. He is the author of *The Theology of Louis Massignon: Islam, Christ, and the Church* (Catholic University of America Press, 2017), and his research interests lie at the intersection of spirituality and Christian-Muslim comparative theology. He has published articles in *Concilium*, *Islam and Christian-Muslim Relations*, *Studies in Interreligious Dialogue*, *Salaam*, and the *Journal of Ecumenical Studies*, among other journals. He is a member of Catholic and Muslim Scholars in Dialogue as well as a series co-editor for *Catholic Theology and Islam* at the Catholic University of America Press.

Leo D. Lefebure is the inaugural holder of the Matteo Ricci, S.J., Chair of Theology at Georgetown University. He is the author of the award-winning *Transforming Interreligious Relations: Catholic Responses to Religious Pluralism in the United States* (Orbis Books, 2020). His other award-winning books include *Revelation, the Religions, and Violence* (Orbis Books, 2000); *True and Holy: Christian Scripture and Other Religions* (Orbis Books, 2013); and *The Path of Wisdom: A Christian Commentary on the Dhammapada* (Eerdmans, 2011), coauthored with Peter Feldmeier. Lefebure is the past president of the Society for Buddhist-Christian Studies, a research fellow of the Chinese University of Hong Kong, and a trustee emeritus of the Council for a Parliament of the World's Religions.

Claude Rault, M. Afr., the bishop of Laghouat (Algeria), is the author of *The Desert Is My Cathedral* (French, Desclée de Brouwer, 2017). Born in Poilley (France) in 1940, he pursued studies in philosophy at the major seminary of Coutances, and in 1966 made his religious profession in the Society of Missionaries of Africa (White Fathers). After studies in Ottawa and Lille he was ordained in 1968 and was later sent to study at the PISAI in Rome (1971–1972). He was appointed to Algeria in 1972 to care for small communities in the south (in the former French

Sahara). In 1979, with Father Christian de Chergé (prior of the monastery of Tibhirine before his assassination in 1996), he founded *Ribāṭ al-salām*, a group of religious and lay people keen to practice Christian-Muslim dialogue, who met twice a year at the Abbey of Nôtre Dame de l'Atlas in Tibhirine. In 1999 Msgr. Rault was appointed provincial of the White Fathers in Algeria and Tunisia. In 2004 he was appointed bishop of Laghouat in Algeria.

Rev. Bonnie Thurston, PhD, formerly a university and seminary professor, resigned a professorship and chair in New Testament to live quietly in her home state, West Virginia, USA. The author or editor of twenty-three books in New Testament studies and spirituality, including *Hidden in God: Discovering the Desert Vision of Charles de Foucauld* (Ave Maria Press, 2016), and six collections of poetry, she recently authored *St. Mary of Egypt: A Modern Verse Life and Interpretation* (Liturgical Press, 2021).

Little Sister Cathy Wright has been a member of the Little Sisters of Jesus since 1973. The Community was founded in the spirituality of Charles de Foucauld in Algeria in 1939 by Little Sister Magdeleine Hutin. Cathy lived nearly thirty years on Chicago's West Side. She is the author of *Saint Charles de Foucauld: His Life and Spirituality* (Pauline Books and Media, 2022).